Yes!
You Can Be
Gay <u>AND</u> Christian!

A collection of sermons that helps you
"experience the unconditional love of God
without the guilt of religion."

by
REVEREND J. R. FINNEY, II
SENIOR PASTOR
COVENANT COMMUNITY CHURCH
BIRMINGHAM, ALABAMA

Yes! You Can Be Gay AND Christian!

Published by J. R. Finney, LLC
Atlanta, GA

ACKNOWLEDGEMENTS

Every attempt has been made to credit the sources of copyrighted material used in this book. If any such acknowledgment has been inadvertently omitted, incorrectly cited, or inaccurately credited, notification of such information would be appreciated.

All scripture quotations, unless otherwise noted, are taken from The Holy Bible, New International Version®.

THE HOLY BIBLE, NEW INTERNATIONAL VERSION®, NIV® Copyright © 1973, 1978, 1984, 2011 by Biblica, Inc.™ Used by permission. All rights reserved worldwide.

Scripture quotations marked (THE MESSAGE) taken from:

THE MESSAGE. **Copyright © 1993, 1994, 1995, 1996, 2000, 2001, 2002. Used by permission of NavPress Publishing Group. All rights reserved.**

Scripture quotations marked (KJV) taken from:

THE HOLY BIBLE – AUTHORIZED KING JAMES VERSION. Copyright © 2003. Used by permission. All rights reserved.

Cover Design by Jake Wade
Photos by Brett Penny
Printed and bound in the United States of America

TABLE OF CONTENTS

INTRODUCTION

Why a book of sermons titled "**Yes! You Can Be Gay <u>and</u> Christian!?**"

The answer is quite simple – to fill a void and to meet a need. Christian bookstores are filled with books of sermons and a plethora of sermons are readily available on the Internet covering practically every conceivable topic from every conceivable Christian persuasion. However, this particular book of sermons is unique; it is written with an unconventional Christian evangelistic purpose in mind. To help you more fully understand my evangelistic purpose, let me share with you two things in the introduction to this book.

First, I want to acquaint you with me as a "Gay Christian Pastor." Through learning about my story, you may understand my passion for wanting the Lesbian/Gay/Bi-Sexual/Transgendered/Questioning (LGBTQ) Community to accept the fact that God knows who they are and still loves them.

Second, I want to share my preaching philosophy that I practice at Covenant Community Church, a very unique Christian congregation. My hope is that, by understanding my preaching philosophy and reading this book of sermons, you will be led to stretch your concepts of who God really is and what God is really like into a wonderful new view of living life to the fullest in fellowship with God.

WHO I AM: I am a Gay Christian Pastor and *"My salvation and my Honor depend on God, He is my mighty rock, my refuge."* (Psalms 62:7).[1]

I am a Christian. I love the Lord, and I know in every facet of my personality and through every fiber of my being that the Lord also loves me. The Lord has blessed me in every good and kind endeavor I have ever undertaken. The Lord has allowed me to see lives changed, hearts mended, and long-held dreams realized just from my obedience in preaching the gospel of God's inclusive love. All of these things have been accomplished through God's work through me, an openly gay Christian Pastor.

Yes, I am gay. I have been all of my life. It is simply the sexual orientation and gift I have been blessed with from God. I never chose this gift, just as heterosexuals never chose their gifted sexual orientation. When I die, I will be absent from the body and immediately present with the Lord as one of God's children who lived most of his entire life openly gay. The reality of my life is simply this: there has never been a time when I was not aware of my attraction to members of my same gender. Although I initially struggled against the attraction, by my early twenties, I knew I was fighting a losing battle. I had tried, with all my might, to change into a heterosexual. I had prayed prayers, attempted to bargain with God, and as the ultimate proof of my "manhood," had completed a successful tour of duty in the U. S. Air Force. Despite my best and sincere efforts, I could not change my sexual

---

[1] All scriptural references in this book are to *The Holy Bible, New International Version*®, unless otherwise noted.

orientation. I then realized that I had one of two choices: 1) I could choose to accept the person that God had made me or 2) I could continue to try to be what society told me I should be (and what I had tried to be with all my might!) In the end, peace only came when I fully accepted the life that had been ordained for me!

I am exceedingly blessed. In the late 1970s when I "came-out" to my parents, they whole-heartedly continued to embrace their gay son, although my mother was apprehensive about my safety. The most beautiful thing for me in coming out to my parents was that I never saw or experienced any difference between the way my parents treated me before or after learning of my sexual orientation. Their reaction to learning of my sexual orientation was, in itself, a great testament to God's love for me and to my parents' understanding of a loving family and true Christian principles. While my father, as a political scientist, held strong intractable opinions about everything, he tended to be rather liberal. On the other hand, my mother was a college educator, preacher, pastor, and diocesan bishop in the very conservative Pentecostal Holiness Church. However, she neither let her education nor her religious beliefs displace her love for me. My parents' unconditional love was an immense gift in my life and I will always be grateful to them and God for that gift.

MY PREACHING PHILOSOPHY: An important insight into my preaching philosophy at Covenant is found in one of the phrases we use when promoting the church in the LGBTQ community. It says, "Come experience the unconditional love of God without the guilt of religion." We are NOT a gay church. We are an unabashedly Christ-centered church that is affirming of all people as we invite them to join us in discovering the love of God as followers of Christ. The nature of our church is reflected in our vision statement: "To be an inclusive community of faith, Offering Hope + Showing Faithfulness + Sharing Joy." Nonetheless, it is true that Covenant Community Church has been called into existence by God with a ministry emphasis to the LGBTQ community, a community that has neither been affirmed by most of the traditional Christian Churches, nor evangelized with the exciting hope of the good news of God's unconditional love.

Each preaching and teaching opportunity at Covenant reflects my overall pastoral philosophy in meeting the spiritual nourishment needs of our congregation, as well as the needs of the larger LGBTQ community. Too many people in the LGBTQ community have shunned their Christian faith heritage. Many members of our community were raised in Christian homes and received otherwise solid Christian upbringings, but were told in their homes, schools, and churches that, based solely on their sexuality, God does not love them and that they are going straight to hell!!!

Even worse, however, is the fact that many members of our community, who do not have Christian upbringings, will not even consider embracing the Christian faith as followers of Christ. Too many members of our community have been religiously "gay-bashed" by those called the "Christian Right." Too many members of our community have been disenfranchised by politicians seeking easy votes by playing to the unwarranted fears of some voters, all supposedly in the name of God. Too many members of our community have been rejected and ostracized by their families and friends, even as those family members and friends held themselves out as models of Christian virtue. Therefore, too many members of the LGBTQ community cannot see any reason why they should embrace Christianity or how Christianity can embrace them.

But there is hope!!

Our community must be given the great message that God has been imparting to humanity from the beginning of time. **God loves us all!!!** In the sermons I preach, I constantly make that point, again and again, in very simple and clear language.

Finally, many have tried to summarize the scriptures this way, *"The Bible is a love story of how the Son of God became a Son of Man, so that the children of humans might become the children of God."* Therefore, my prayer and the ultimate evangelistic purpose of this book is that, as you read these sermons, you will begin to accept God's love or have your faith journey renewed by the power and knowledge of God's great love for you.

Rev. J.R. Finney, II

DEDICATION

This book of sermons is lovingly dedicated to the memory of my dear parents--Jack and James Ella Reid Finney, whose unconditional love for me modeled and foreshadowed the unconditional love that I would come to know from God.

I am also grateful to the members and friends of Covenant Community Church in Birmingham, Alabama, whose impact on my life could never be overstated. Many thanks for the loving and gracious manner in which you have treated me, while allowing me to serve as your pastor since September 2000.

A special note of thanks certainly goes to former Deacon Greg Adams of Covenant Community Church. The bold and positive statement--*"Yes! You can be Gay and Christian!"*--which appropriately serves as both the title of this book and the title of the anchor sermon, was an epiphany to him for the theme of Covenant's float for the Pride Parade of June 2005.

I also owe a huge debt of gratitude to Bryndis Roberts for her tireless editing and sincere appreciation to Jennifer Jenkins and Gérard Erdue for proofing this book. Finally, to my dear friend, William Jenkins, whose encouragement and shepherding of this project took it from being just a good idea to a reality, thanks for believing in this endeavor!

PART I:
GAY PRIDE SERMONS

"Always be prepared to give an answer to everyone who asks you to give the reason for the hope that you have. But do this with gentleness and respect..." I Peter 3:15[2]

The sermons included in Part I were all preached on Sunday mornings just prior to our congregation joining the rest of the LGBTQ Community for the annual PrideFest celebrations in Birmingham, Alabama. The aim of these sermons was to take this unique opportunity each year, with the large gathering of LGBTQ people, to encourage and exhort the members and friends of Covenant to allow God to use us in sharing our hope (***"with gentleness and respect"***) of making a positive difference in God's Kingdom as well as in the lives of other people.

---

[2] The scriptural lesson for each sermon is printed at the beginning of each chapter. No further citations are made in the body of the sermon when any references are made to or quotations are included of any of the scriptures that are part of the scriptural lesson.

CHAPTER 1: YES!
YOU CAN BE GAY AND CHRISTIAN!

A sermon using the following scriptures:

Epistle Text: Romans 5:1-5

¹Therefore, since we have been justified through faith, we have peace with God through our Lord Jesus Christ, ²through whom we have gained access by faith into this grace in which we now stand. And we rejoice in the hope of the glory of God. ³Not only so, but we also rejoice in our sufferings, because we know that suffering produces perseverance; ⁴perseverance, character; and character, hope. ⁵And hope does not disappoint us, because God has poured out his love into our hearts by the Holy Spirit, whom he has given us.

Gospel Text: Matthew 9:35-38

³⁵Jesus went through all the towns and villages, teaching in their synagogues, preaching the good news of the kingdom and healing every disease and sickness. ³⁶When [Jesus] saw the crowds, He had compassion on them, because they were harassed and helpless, like sheep without a shepherd. ³⁷Then [Jesus] said to his disciples, "The harvest is plentiful but the workers are few. ³⁸Ask the Lord of the harvest, therefore, to send out workers into His harvest field."

THE SERMON

Happy Pride Sunday! Today, we will gather with folks from all over our community to celebrate PrideFest[3] for Central Alabama. As we do, I hope you, the people of Covenant Community Church, will remember our ministry vision for this year. That vision is *"Restoring that which is lost by 'Offering Hope + Showing Faithfulness + Sharing Joy.'"*

We go to PrideFest to celebrate liberation, to honor those who have gone before us in our struggle for equality and, as Christians, we go as living examples of the unconditional love of God. We also go to proclaim a powerful message to our community: **YES! YOU CAN BE GAY AND CHRISTIAN!!**

Today's quotes come from three lesbian comediennes. The first quote comes from Robin Tyler: *"If homosexuality is a disease, let's all call in queer to work: 'Hello, can't work today, still queer.'"* The second quote comes from Rita Mae Brown: *"My lesbianism is an act of Christian Charity. All those women out there praying for a man, I'm giving them my share."* The third quote is the famous one by Lynn Lavner: *"The Bible contains six admonishments to homosexuals and 362 admonishments to heterosexuals. That doesn't mean God doesn't love heterosexuals. It's just that they need more supervision."*

---

[3] "PrideFest" is the annual Pride celebrations of Gays, Lesbians, Bisexuals, Transgendered persons, and others, held in the city of Birmingham and throughout Central Alabama.

As I stated earlier, we have a message to proclaim to our community. That message, which is the theme of our Pride activities this year and the title of this sermon, is "**Yes! You Can Be Gay and Christian!**" That theme is the brain child of Deacon Greg Adams who was in charge of our Pride floats. It was an epiphany to him earlier this year as he was giving thought to our Pride float.

Wow! What an absolutely great theme. Thank you, Greg! That theme encapsulates everything we want to say to our community on this Pride Sunday for Central Alabama. The Gospel of Matthew says it so well: *When [Jesus] saw the crowds, He had compassion on them, because they were harassed and helpless, like sheep without a shepherd. Then [Jesus] said to his disciples, 'The harvest is plentiful but the workers are few. Ask the Lord of the harvest, therefore, to send out workers into His harvest field.'*

As we go into our community today, we go as workers in the harvest fields of God with a message to our community that "**Yes! You Can be Gay and Christian!**" It is a bold message. It is a message that is difficult for some members of our community to accept or even contemplate, because they have been harassed and their faith has been made helpless by the loud and disparaging voices of those who dare to claim they speak for God while telling our people they cannot be a part of God's family.

Therefore, we must speak loudly with our presence, our love for God, and the hope in our lives, so that by God's grace, people can hear the message we bring. That message is:

Yes! You can be Gay and Christian because "the Word of God says so!"

One of the most familiar passages in the entire Bible is John 3:16. You even see these big signs in the bleachers at football games with only one thing on them – John 3:16. That's how widespread the recognition of that verse is. It's the Word of God.

When other voices are shouting to our community that we CANNOT be a part of God's family, we must raise our voices and shout, "Yes! You can be gay and Christian because the Word of God says so!" John 3:16 says, *"For God so loved the world, that [God gave God's only begotten, Jesus], that whosoever believeth in Him should not perish, but have everlasting life."* (KJV). That scripture does not say *"whosoever, except."* Instead, that powerful scripture simply says clearly and unequivocally, *"whosoever."* That word – *whosoever* – includes you, me and anyone else who believes. **"Yes! You can be Gay and Christian"** because the Word of God says so!"

Yes! You can be Gay and Christian, because "my own Christian experience tells me so!"

Many of you have heard me say on numerous occasions, *"Trust your own integrity!"* Unfortunately, too often members of our community hear messages such as:

> "No, you cannot be a Christian and gay;"
> "No, you cannot be a part of God's family;"
> "No, you cannot be a part of our Church;" or
> "You are an abomination to God."

When all we hear are those negative, hurtful messages, a lot of us begin to believe them and start to doubt our own integrity. So, when someone comes along and says to our community --**"Yes! You can be Gay and Christian!"**— many members of our community find that good news hard to believe and some of them are even offended.

You have to learn to trust your own integrity, even in the face of those negative messages that keep playing in your mind. You know in your heart whether you believe in Jesus Christ. You know whether you were sincere when you asked Jesus Christ to come into your heart and your life as Savior, Lord and Sovereign. So trust your own integrity. That is what I had to learn to do.

On Wednesday night we previewed the short documentary that film-maker Clay Daniels made about Covenant called *"The Congregation."* In that documentary I said, *"The Bible says that whoever calls on the name of the Lord, shall be saved. I called on the Lord, I asked Jesus Christ to come into my life. I am saved and that is the end of that discussion."* I repeat that declaration to you today. The words of the Bible tell me that I am saved! Because of God's word and my own personal experience, I can go into our community today with confidence in knowing that **"Yes! You can be Gay and Christian!"** because my own Christian experience tells me so!"

Yes! You can be Gay and Christian, because changed lives at Covenant proclaim it so!

I wish I had about an hour to talk on this topic because the examples here at Covenant – when I stop and think about them – just overwhelm me.   But I only have a few moments.

A relatively new worshipper at Covenant, Diane, is serving as our acolyte today. Diane and her partner, Chelsea, came to us on a Wednesday night. Chelsea was always very outgoing, but Diane was quite introverted. Life and family had not always been kind to her. But here at Covenant, we have watched her life change so dramatically in the last year. When she initially came to us, she would have never been bold enough to serve as an acolyte, as a greeter, and as an usher. She never would have been brave enough to be a volunteer for us at *Grace by Day.*[4] Diane, we love you, and you are a great example that **"Yes! You can be Gay and Christian!"** because your changed life here at Covenant proclaims it so!

This past Wednesday, I attended the Gay Pride Town Hall Meeting.[5] At the meeting, the question that was the focal point of our discussion was *"why should the discussion of faith be included in our community?"* My answer was because of the hope it brings. That answer came from the Epistle lectionary that I had just read prior to that event. Hope is not something you can experience with the five

---

[4] *Grace by Day* is a mid-day hospitality ministry in which Covenant partners with Grace Episcopal Church in Woodlawn (a community in Birmingham, Alabama) to provide services to the homeless and other people in need in the Birmingham area.

[5] The "Gay Pride Town Hall Meeting" is an annual event sponsored by Equality Alabama (a civil rights organization focused on LGBTQ issues) during Central Alabama Pride Week. The event seeks to foster a community discussion of issues facing LGBTQ people in Alabama.

senses. It is a longing that is deeper than any of our five senses can recognize.

Today, as we participate in PrideFest, we will meet people who are longing for hope in their lives. Sadly, many of them will not know that what they are longing for is a relationship with God. They will not know it because all they have ever heard is that because they are gay, bi-sexual, lesbian, or transgendered, they cannot have a relationship with God. As a result, many of them have given up any hope of ever having an ongoing, loving, and healthy relationship with God. Today, remember that we are workers in the harvest. We must proclaim hope, because *"hope does not disappoint us . . . God has poured out [God's] love into our hearts by the Holy Spirit . . ."*

We go forward today to help restore hope to the members of our community. We boldly proclaim the message that **"Yes! You can be Gay and Christian!!"** The Word of God says so, my own Christian experience tells me so, and changed lives here at Covenant proclaim it so. Why? There is a little chorus that says, *"People need the Lord, at the end of broken dreams, He's the open door. When will we realize. . .that people need the Lord?"*[6]

---

[6] Nelson, Greg and Phill McHugh (Words and Music). "People Need the Lord." Lyrics. Shepherd's Fold Music/River Oaks Music Co. (both administered by EMI Christian Music Publishing), 1983 and 2006.

CHAPTER 2: ONE IN CHRIST
AND UNITED FOR EQUALITY
(The Truth That Sets Us Free)

A sermon using the following scriptures:

The Epistle Text: Galatians 3:23 - 28
[23]Before this faith came, we were held prisoners by the law, locked up until faith should be revealed. [24]So the law was put in charge to lead us to Christ that we might be justified by faith. [25]Now that faith has come, we are no longer under the supervision of the law. [26]You are all [children] of God through faith in Christ Jesus, [27]for all of you who were baptized into Christ have clothed yourselves with Christ. [28]There is neither Jew nor Greek, slave nor free, male nor female, for you are all one in Christ Jesus.

The Gospel Text: John 3:17
"For God did not send [Christ] into the world to condemn the world, but to save the world through [Christ]."

John 8:31 - 36
[31]To the Jews who had believed him, Jesus said, "If you hold to my teaching, you are really my disciples. [32]Then you will know the truth, and the truth will set you free." [33]They answered him, "We are Abraham's descendants and have never been slaves of anyone. How can you say that we shall be set free?" [34]Jesus replied, "I tell you the truth, everyone who sins is a slave to sin. [35]Now a slave has no permanent place in the family, but a son belongs to it forever. [36]So if the Son sets you free, you will be free indeed."

THE SERMON

All around the world, during the month of June, the LGBTQ community celebrates PrideFest. Most of the celebrations last for a number of days, usually culminating with major events on "Pride Sunday." Regrettably, for too many of us in our community, these pride celebrations are the only time during the year when we feel like we have a voice, that we have a family, and that we are loved for our true selves.

The word "pride" is sort of a double-edged sword. It can be a very good thing; on the other hand, it can also be a bad thing. So, let me make my meaning clear. When I speak of pride, I am not talking about it in its meaning of *"arrogance or disdainful conduct or treatment."* The Pride I am speaking of, and the Pride that we are celebrating in our LGBTQ community, is that of *"gaining a sense of proper dignity, value and self-respect."* This type of Pride is simply the "self-worth" that God intended for each of God's children.

The PrideFest theme this year is "**United for Equality**." As a church, Covenant has a God-given purpose of being united with the rest of our community as, together, we strive for equality. But to be a successful partner with our community means that we must first be united in purpose here. W*e must learn to be one in Christ here* in our church before we go into our community. So on this Pride Sunday, before we go to join our community in celebrating Pride, let me first speak to you about us as a church being **"One in Christ and United for Equality**."

Since today is Pride Sunday, I thought I would share some Pride T-shirt "truths that will set you free." **I found these on the Internet and I thought you should consider them:**

1) *God made me gay. Unity made me proud. America made me second class!*
2) *Will God judge me for loving or judge you for hating?!*
3) *God is good. God is great. God made me gay instead of straight!*

As you go about your week beyond today's Pride celebration, I encourage you to take some time to think about these great T-shirt truths for their logic contains *"the truth that can set us free."*

Scripted across libraries all over the world is that partial scripture from John 8:32 *"...the truth will set you free."* It is a partial scriptural text and it is also a partial truth. The whole scriptural thought starts in verse 31, where Jesus says, *"If you hold to My teaching, you are really My disciples. Then you will know the truth and the truth will set you free."* The truth will only set you free if you know it and then embrace it. So this Pride Sunday, I want you to know the truth, to embrace the truth, and to let the truth set you free. And, w*hat is the truth?*

The first part of the truth is a message that you and I need desperately to hear on this Pride Sunday. <u>The message is that Jesus Christ can help us reach our full potential</u>. Yes, we have our flaws; many of us have not lived our best lives, and many of us have made terrible mistakes in our lives. Many of those mistakes occurred because society and the church told us we were not normal *(whatever that is)*. Consequently, so many of us were made to believe that we could not have a relationship with God. That damnable assertion has caused many of us to settle for less than God's best in our lives and it has also caused many of us to fail to recognize what God can make of our lives.

Too often church folks have abused our community as a means to cover and mask their own shortcomings. I was reading a story told about the late writer and poet, Dorothy Parker, who was known for her sarcastic wit. She was at a rather snooty cocktail party and one of the guests said to Dorothy of another guest at the party, **"Isn't she something? You know dear, she is so very kind to her inferiors."** With mock disbelief, Dorothy Parker asked, *"And where does she find them?"*

Stripped of its sarcasm, her point is well made. There are no "superiors'" in God's world; nor are there any "inferiors." There are only people -- precious people -- and we are part of those people and all of us have potential. *Why?* It is because we are fashioned by our Creator God to have potential.

Make no mistake about it. Although your potential is different from mine and mine is different from the next person, we all are remarkably valuable in God's sight. The truth that sets us free on this Pride Sunday is that there are no big *'I's* and little *'U's*. Here at Covenant, *"we are one in Christ."* Paul reminds us of that principle today in the Epistle lesson when he says, *"[t]here is neither Jew nor Greek, slave nor free, male nor female,* (and I will just add there is neither straight nor gay) *for [we] are all one in Christ Jesus!* That principle is a truth that will set us free this Pride Sunday and will enable us to go forward being **"One in Christ and United for Equality."**

The second part of the truth is that if we believe in Christ, we must value each and every one of God's Children. As a Christian church, we at Covenant believe there are no excuses for anyone to put up roadblocks to keep any child of God from experiencing the unconditional love of God.

My Mama's favorite pope, Pope John XXIII, made a statement that says exactly what I am trying to say to you today. He said: **"When people are animated by the love of Christ, they feel united and the needs, sufferings and joys of others are felt as their own. Love unites us."** You see, Pope John XXIII understood, as we at Covenant seek to understand, that we must value every one of God's children because, after all, we are all one in Christ. The truth that sets us free on this Pride Sunday is that by valuing each and every person, we have no choice but to be **"One in Christ and United for Equality!"**

Finally, the third part of the truth is that we must encourage our community, just as Christ encourages us. That principle is the heart of the Christian faith. That principle is the very center of our Covenant call and the core reason we join our community at PrideFest on this Pride Sunday. John 3:17 tells us *"[f]or God did not send [Christ] into the world to condemn the world, but to save the world through him."* I wish the Christian Church, as a whole, would learn that when we condemn others, for whatever reason, we are not of the mind of Christ. Christians are to encourage others regardless of who they are, just as Christ encourages us. That principle is the overriding thought that I pray each of us will go forth with on this Pride Sunday. Covenant, it is important that, as one in Christ, we unite with our community for equality, but it is even more important that we encourage others today as Christ encourages us.

The modern era Civil Rights movement for equality began right here in Alabama when the late Rosa Parks refused to stand up and give up her seat on a Montgomery bus. Years later, Rosa Parks was asked why she would not stand when ordered. She responded **"it was because of my mother and my Christian upbringing. I was brought up to believe in freedom and equality and that <u>God designs all His children to be free</u>."**

Covenant, as a church, we are "**One in Christ**," and today, as every day, we stand with our community "**United for Equality**" because we believe that **"God designs all His children to be free."** We need to share with our community that God has designed them to be free and they should never be satisfied living as second class citizens.

This Sunday is Pride Sunday. Covenant, today we go forth as "**One in Christ and United for Equality**" because **it is time for our community to experience a Christian Church like Covenant that:**

1) **Sees the potential in our community, as Christ sees the great potential in each of us. It makes**

**no difference how they look or where they come
from.**

2) **Recognizes their value as God's children; and**
3) **Offers real encouragement to them as Christ
encourages us.**

This Sunday is Pride Sunday! Let us go forth and make a difference in our community *with the unconditional love of Christ without the guilt of religion*. But, before we go, let us remind ourselves that we are *"One in Christ and United for Equality"* because <u>we are one in the bond of love</u>. It is the truth that will set us free!

CHAPTER 3: PROUD TO BE A WHOSOEVER

A sermon using the following scriptures:

The Epistle Text: Romans 8:14-16
[T]hose who are led by the Spirit of God are sons of God. *For you did not receive a spirit that makes you a slave again to fear, but you received the Spirit of [daughterhood and] sonship. And by him we cry, "Abba, Father."* *The Spirit himself testifies with our spirit that we are God's children.*

The Gospel Text: John 3:16
For God so loved the world, that he gave his only begotten Son, that whosoever believes in him should not perish, but have everlasting life. (New King James Version).

THE SERMON

Happy Pride Sunday!   This week, here in Birmingham, I felt like I was caught in the opening lines of *A Tale of Two Cities*, by Charles Dickens, in which he says, "It was the best of times and the worst of times." It was the best of times because for the first time in the history of Alabama, an out lesbian, Patricia Todd, came in first in her district race for the state legislative. If she wins in the run-off, she will become the first openly gay legislator in Alabama state government history![7]   But it has also been the worst of

---

[7]Patricia Todd was victorious in the run-off, making her the first openly gay legislator in Alabama state government history!

times. This week that awful, hateful, mean-spirited Amendment One was passed overwhelmingly by the voters of this state, as *Alabama seeks to enshrine – once again -- an article of discrimination in its constitution. How sad!* How very sad! As most of you know, Amendment One prohibits the recognition of marriages between persons of the same gender.

But on this Pride Sunday, I am reminded of what one noted civil rights activist once proclaimed when he said that, in this fight, "**My head may get bloodied, but my knees will NOT bow to oppression and discrimination.**"[8] Because of this latest example of oppression and discrimination, I want to proclaim, on this Pride Sunday, that I am "**Proud to be a Whosoever!**"

While thinking about the passage of that evil Amendment One, I found on the Internet where someone had (rather tongue in cheek) put together a list of humorous thoughts on gay marriage to show how irrational the arguments against gay marriage are. Here are my top five points from that list:

1) Obviously gay parents will raise gay children. After all we all know straight parents only raise straight children. **NOT!**
2) If we allow gay marriage, then straight marriage, such as Britney Spears' 55-hour, just-for-fun marriage, will be less meaningful in our society. **NOT!**

---

[8] Quotes from the sayings of Dr. Martin Luther King, Jr., a variation of a line from the poem "*Invictus*" by William Ernest Henley.

3) Gay marriage should be decided by people not the courts, because after all, we all know that majority-elected legislatures, and not courts, have historically done a wonderful job of protecting the rights of the minorities. **NOT!**

4) Civil unions, providing most of the same benefits as marriage with a different name, are preferable, because separate-but-equal institutions in America are constitutional. **NOT!**

5) Gay marriage will encourage people to be gay, in the same way that hanging around tall people will make you tall. **NOT!**

On a more serious note, I was especially saddened that these efforts of discrimination are being lead by Christians! But God always knows what we need and my spirit received some much needed encouragement from this week's lectionary readings. The scriptures made me **"Proud to be a Whosoever."** In Romans, Paul tells us that **"those who are led by the Spirit of God are children of God. For we did not receive a spirit that makes us slaves again to fear, but we received the Spirit of [daughterhood and] sonship."** I am a child of God! No one can decide that but God and me. I made the decision as my part of the equation when I accepted the salvation Christ purchased on Calvary. God made the decision on His side of the equation when Christ accepted my confession and invitation to come into my life as my Lord and Savior. That is it!

I know that many of us have been deeply hurt by what preachers preach and by what churches teach and do. As I have often stated, however, we must be careful and **"not**

necessarily equate the church with God!" God is perfect! However, the church, because of those who attend it, is far from being perfect! The fact that you have any desire whatsoever to be here in worship is in itself proof that you are being led by the Spirit of God.

John's gospel says, **"For God so loved the world, that [God] gave [God's] only begotten Son, that whosoever believes in [Jesus] should not perish, but have everlasting life."** That scripture is the entire gospel in one verse and it tells us everything we need to know to be-- **"Proud to be a Whosoever"**--secure in the knowledge that we are children of God.

First of all, that scripture tells us of the love of God. I have never been able to understand or agree with those preachers who continually dwell on the wrath of God. They seem to take some kind of sadistic delight in trying to scare the hell out of people by proclaiming the wrath and punishment of God, even though the whole message of the Bible is condensed in the first six words of John 3:16: **"For God so loved the world . . ."** The key to understanding God is the fact that God loves! God loves each and every one of us as if each of us was God's only child to love!

Listening to what some preaches preach and some churches teach, it is easy to think of God as looking down on us and just waiting for us to make a mistake. It is easy to believe that God is some kind of vengeful God who is going to punish us when we step out of line. But the tremendous thing about this Gospel is that, in one verse, it makes me **"Proud to Be a Whosoever"** because it affirms that God loves you and me simply because we are God's children!

The little children's song got it right, **"[r]ed and yellow, black and white, [we all] are precious in [God's] sight."**[9] On this Pride Sunday, I want you to go out of here knowing that God loves you. You are God's child! Hold your head high and be - **"Proud to be a Whosoever."**

Second, that scripture assures me of the gift of God. The gift of God is **God's presence in this world through Jesus Christ.** John says, **"the Word became flesh and dwelt among us . . . full of grace & truth."**[10] God's gift is that we are not alone – God is with us, because of Christ.

As part of our Pride Celebrations, we held our annual Town Hall meeting on Wednesday evening. After the Town Hall meeting, a young man approached me and told me how much he appreciated my remarks, especially about faith. He grew up in the church and wants so badly to have a relationship with God. But the church has been very cruel to him and he finds himself getting bitter because of the way he has been treated by the church. I told him what I said earlier, **"do not equate the church with God. Often the two have nothing in common."**

This young man and I are intending to meet soon and to have a lengthy conversation about faith issues. The points I am making in this message are some of the thoughts I will be sharing with him. He needs the affirmation of God's

---

[9] Root, George Frederick (1820-1895) (Music) and C. Herbert Woolston (1856-1927) (Lyrics). "Jesus Loves the Little Children." Public Domain.

[10] John 1:14 (King James Version).

gift in his life; he needs to be **"Proud to be a Whosoever,"** knowing that God's presence is with him always.

Finally, that scripture proclaims to us the promise of God. The promise is **"...that whosoever believes in [Jesus] should not perish, but have everlasting life."** Too many of us think that everlasting life begins after you are pushing up daisies, but not so. Everlasting life occurs the moment we accept Christ as our Savior and Sovereign, and it lasts forever. The Apostle Paul affirms this in Romans 14:8, when he says, **"whether we live or die, we are the Lord's."**

Yes, preachers will continue to preach discrimination to try to keep us isolated from God. Yes, churches will continue to teach discrimination to try to keep us isolated from the rest of society. And, yes, state legislatures will continue to enact new laws to deny us equal legal rights. Despite these actions, there are some truths that preachers, churches, and state legislatures cannot change. Truths such as: **"Those who are led by the Spirit of God are children of God. For we did not receive a spirit that makes us slaves again to fear, but we received the Spirit of [daughterhood and] sonship." "For God so loved the world, that [God] gave [God's] only begotten Son, that whosoever believes in [Jesus] should not perish, but have everlasting life."** So **"whether we live or die, we are the Lord's."** These scriptures are eternal truths and God, the author and finisher of our faith, has the final word.

Many of us will go to PrideFest today. My advice on this Pride Sunday is for you to go **"Proud to Be a Whosoever."** Doing so has eternal benefits for you and, potentially, eternal benefits for those you come in contact with today. By being **"Proud to Be a Whosoever,"** you become part of God's love, God's gift, God's promise, and God's plan for our community to become reconciled to the fact that they are God's children too! As God's children, we are loved by God with the same fervor with which God loves everyone else!

So let us go to **PrideFest** today **"Proud to Be Whosoevers"** because people need to know about our faith in God and because people need to know that they are God's children. That urge that brought you here today can be used by God to make a positive difference in someone else's life today!

PART II:
THE NATURE OF
GOD'S LOVE

"The love of God is greater far
Than tongue or men could ever tell,
It goes beyond the highest star
And reaches to the lowest hell."

From the Lyrics of *"The Love of God"* written by Frederick M. Lehman.[11]

The sermons in Part II reach out to people in our community who have walked in condemnation for so long that they find themselves spiritually and mentally in what they might describe as ***"the lowest hell."*** Such condemnation has often made them think that "God loving them" is beyond the realm of possibility for their lives. These sermons were designed to help our community see ***"the Nature of God's love."*** My belief is that as people come to know the truth about ***"the Nature of God's love,"*** they will come to believe in and trust in the fact that God does indeed love them.

---

[11] Lehman, Frederick M. (Words and Music)(1868-1953) and Claudia Faustina Lehman Mays (Harmonization) "The Love of God." Public Domain, 1917.

CHAPTER 4: SO YOU WANT TO KNOW ABOUT TRUE LOVE?

A sermon using the following scriptures:

The Epistle Text: I John 3:1-3
[1]How great is the love the Father has lavished on us, that we should be called children of God! And that is what we are! The reason the world does not know us is that it did not know him. [2]Dear friends, now we are children of God, and what we will be has not yet been made known. But we know that when he appears, we shall be like him, for we shall see him as he is. [3]Everyone who has this hope in him purifies himself, just as he is pure.

The Gospel Text: **John 13:34-35**
[34]"A new command I give you: Love one another. As I have loved you, so you must love one another. [35]By this all [people] will know that you are my disciples, if you love one another." (Inclusiveness added)

THE SERMON

This Sunday is one of those Sundays when there are so many things going on that it is hard to cover them all in one sermon. It is not only the sixth Sunday after Epiphany, but it is also *"Black History Month."*

As is our custom here at Covenant, each year, during Black History Month, we pause to honor a person who has made significant positive contributions to the issue of Civil Rights for people of this country. This year we honor Dr. Joseph Lowery for his support and commitment to the

Civil Rights of minorities and, in particular, for his support and commitment to members of the LGBTQ community. Dr. Lowery insists, (and rightfully so, I might add), that LGBTQ folks be included in God's Christian family.

Today is also our once a quarter *"Bring-A-Friend" Sunday*, and we are certainly happy that many of you brought a friend to join us in our worship services today. Additionally, today we have visiting with us the wonderful gay comedian, Ant, accompanied by a Logo Television filming crew. Finally, in addition to all of those activities, this coming Tuesday will be Valentine's Day. So if you have a significant other, make sure you don't forget how important that person is to you. Indeed, we have a lot to celebrate and commemorate today!!

Have you ever pretended you were someone else? Many LGBTQ people have. Often that action has been the result of being gay and having experienced the disapproval, rejection, scorn, and ostracism of being who we are. Maybe that rejection caused some of us to wish we were someone else. I think some of us pretend to be someone else because all we want is to know true love from our family, our friends, or maybe that special someone in our lives. Fearing rejection for who we really are, we think that if we could just be someone else, just for the weekend, just through the holidays, or just for a little while, maybe we could find that acceptance, that true love that we are seeking. Today let's consider the question, ***"So, You want to know about true love?"***

In speaking of "true love," you may remember that some weeks ago in the morning sermon I told you that God thinks that each one of us is somebody. I also told you that when I was growing up, my Mama and Daddy told me I was somebody and whether they were telling me the truth or a lie, I chose to believe them!!! Then after service, someone (a "nemesis" of mine) who shall remain nameless, told me that my Mama may have lied to me to keep from hurting my feelings. Of course you know he will live to regret that comment!

Of course, my friend was only joking with me . . . I think. And, even if I thought for one moment that he had not been joking, I would still choose to believe my Mama and Daddy. You see, I know I am somebody!! I also know that loads and loads of hurt, pain, and conflict would be eliminated from our lives if each member of our community learned to appreciate and proclaim his or her true identity – I am SOMEBODY! One of the greatest contributions to the Civil Rights Movement came when Reverend Jesse Jackson led marchers with the chant: I am SOMEBODY! It would be a life-changing event for many within our LGBTQ community if we could stand up and say, **"This person is who I am, and nothing you say or do can detract from that fact."** Imagine how great it would be if our people experienced that kind of true love from themselves and others! So, let us talk about true love, looking at three principles.

First, true love starts with knowing who you are.

It is simple. Often, we do not know true love because we do not know who we are and whose we are. In one of the questions posed by Dr. Joseph Lowery, he asks how could the church, because of a person's sexual orientation, deny ministry to those whom God has called?

The point is this: You are called by God! The Epistle lesson today says, *"How great is the love [God] has lavished on us, that we should be called children of God! And that is what we are!"* God wants us to know who we are. God wants us to know and realize that we too are children of God. That knowledge is how you come to know and experience true love. You do so by coming to know and believe that you are a beloved child of God! This knowledge is so powerful that once you accept and come to believe it, your life will change, your attitude about yourself will change, and your actions towards others will change. There would be no desire to be someone else. There would be no need to be someone else, even for a short time.

Such a wonderful difference would exist in our perspectives on life and love if we really believed and knew the true love of being a child of God, wholly unique, precious, and blessed with a true love we can never lose. So you want to know about true love? True loves starts with knowing who you are.

Second, true love--Christ-like love--is secure.

God wants each of us to experience God's true love because it's secure. It will not let go. In his book, *The Promises of Grace: Living in the Grips of God's Love,*[12] Bryan Chapell writes about that kind of love. He reminds

---

[12] Chapell, Bryan. *The Promises of Grace: Living in the Grips of God's Love.* Michigan: Baker House, 1992, 2001, p. 148.

us of the events surrounding the crash of Northwest Airlines Flight 225.

On Sunday, August 16, 1987, Northwest Flight 225 crashed just after taking off from the Detroit, Michigan, airport. There were 155 people killed in that crash. Only one person survived. The sole survivor was four year old Cecelia Chican. In the aftermath of the crash, many struggled to explain how this four year old little girl could have survived a crash that took the lives of so many adult men, women, and older children, including Cecelia's mother, father, and six year old brother. One of the explanations offered (apparently by one of the first responders to the crash) was that, sensing the imminent crash, Cecilia's mother had unbuckled her own seat belt, gotten down on her knees in front of her daughter, wrapped her arms and body around Cecelia, and then would not let go! No one really knows whether this did or did not happen, but when this story was first reported, it touched the hearts of millions of people around the world!

The final report[13] on the investigation of the crash by the Federal Aviation Administration seems to make it unlikely that the mother could have taken that action; but, whether it happened or not, I believe that the initial reports, contemplating such loving actions on behalf of a mother, touched the hearts of millions because it reminds us of God's love for us. The image painted of this mother's love for her child is like the image of God's love for each of us.

---

[13] *The New York Times*, "Mother May Not Have Saved Lone Survivor of Plane Crash," November 23, 1987, http://www.nytimes.com/1987/11/23/us/mother-may-not-have-saved-...

You see, God wraps God's arms and body around each of us, God's children, and God will not let go!

It is impossible for me to overstate how much GOD loves you. People in this world may have disapproved of you, rejected you, and ostracized you. It may have even gotten so bad that, at times, you wished you were somebody else just to alleviate the pain. But I have come to tell you, proclaim to you, and shout to you about the absolute unconditional love that God has for you! It is a genuine true love that nothing in this world can break. It is a true love that enfolds you in times of crisis. It is a true love that enfolds you in times of rejection and loneliness. It is a true love that never lets go! So you want to know about true love? True love, Christ-like love, is secure.

Third and finally, true love is supportive.

Most of you know that our philosophy around this church is that when God gives to you or when God blesses you, it is not all about you! God expects you to pass your gift or your blessing on to someone else. Sharing our gifts and our blessings with others is the way true Christ-like love works. It is supportive and it offers words of encouragement and hope. It builds up--it does not tear down. The gospel today says *"[a] new command I give you: Love one another. . ."* Part of loving one another is offering words of encouragement and hope to one another.

I am reminded of a story I once heard about a famous coach who had this unique ability to give his players unforgettable words of encouragement when they needed it most. If a player had a great game, usually all that player heard from the coach was "nice game." But if that player had a bad game or was really down and struggling, the coach would be there to comfort, help, and inspire that player. One day, one of the players asked the coach about this routine. The wise coach explained that after a player had played a great game, or scored the winning points, that player is everyone's hero: all of the fans cheer for you, all of the teammates pat you on the back and give you "high fives," and all of the reporters want to interview you. At that moment, you don't need your coach. **You need your coach when nobody else is cheering for you!**

Many of us know what it is like to be down and struggling at times in our lives and have no one cheering for us. Many of us know the hurt and loneliness that we experience when we think, rightfully or wrongfully, that we do not have a friend in this world. Because of those feelings we need to experience the true love of God, so that we can know whose we are. As we read in the Epistle Text, *"[h]ow great is the love that [God] has lavished on us, that we should be called the children of God! And that is what we are!"*

God wants us to know that we are children of God so that when no one is cheering, we are still secure in the true love of God. God also wants us to love one another. Loving one another means we pass on true love through our words of encouragement and our actions toward one another. *"A new command I give you: Love one another. . ."*

So you want to know about true love? Well, the songwriter told us about it in these words:

The love of God is greater far,
Than tongue or pen can ever tell,
It goes beyond the highest star,
And reaches to the lowest hell,

. . . .

O love of God, how rich and pure!
How measureless and strong!
It shall forevermore endure
The saints' and angels' song.[14]

SUMMARY

So, you want to know about true love? Well, look no further than to God. God offers each of us true love. **True love starts with knowing who we are.** It comes from our understanding that we are indeed children of God. **True love, Christ-like love, is a secure love** that wraps itself around us, and no matter what the crisis, refuses to let go. **Finally, true love is supportive.** Even when no one else is cheering for us, God lets us know that God is cheering for us.

---

[14] Lehman, Frederick M. (Words and Music)(1868-1953) and Claudia Faustina Lehman Mays (Harmonization). *"The Love of God."* Public Domain, 1917.

CHAPTER 5: GOD IS LIKE – A MOTHER'S LOVE

A sermon using the following scriptures:

The Epistle Text: Philippians 3:17-21 & 4:1

[17]Join with others in following my example, brothers, and take note of those who live according to the pattern we gave you. [18]For, as I have often told you before and now say again even with tears, many live as enemies of the cross of Christ. [19]Their destiny is destruction, their god is their stomach, and their glory is in their shame. Their mind is on earthly things. [20]But our citizenship is in heaven. And we eagerly await a Savior from there, the Lord Jesus Christ, [21]who, by the power that enables him to bring everything under his control, will transform our lowly bodies so that they will be like his glorious body.

Ch. 4:1 Therefore, my brothers, you whom I love and long for, my joy and crown, that is how you should stand firm in the Lord, dear friends!

The Gospel Text: Luke 13:31-35

[31]At that time some Pharisees came to Jesus and said to him, "Leave this place and go somewhere else. Herod wants to kill you." [32]He replied, "Go tell that fox, 'I will drive out demons and heal people today and tomorrow, and on the third day I will reach my goal.' [33]In any case, I must keep going today and tomorrow and the next day – for surely no prophet can die outside Jerusalem! [34]"O Jerusalem, Jerusalem, you who kill the prophets and stone those sent to you, how often I have longed to gather your children together, as a hen gathers her chicks under her

wings, but you were not willing! ³⁵*Look, your house is left to you desolate. I tell you, you will not see me again until you say, 'Blessed is he who comes in the name of the Lord.'"*

THE SERMON

What is God like? At some point in our Christian lives, most of us ask ourselves that question. We long to know God in a more "human" way. We want to be able to see God, touch God, and have a back and forth conversation with God. We want to know, firsthand and instantly, whether or not God approves or disapproves of the choices we have made in our lives.

Today is the second Sunday of Lent and it is also the first Sunday of Women's History Month. I think it is interesting that the lectionary gospel for today gives us a feminine image of God. Practically all the images of God that most of us grew up with were masculine images. Most people think that God is a man. The Bible most often refers to God as, **"He, Him, Father,"** and so on. A few years ago, it was reported that the Southern Baptist Convention actually voted and decided that God is a man. *(If that report is true, bless their hearts.)*

However, in the gospel lesson today, Jesus used an uncommon view of God to demonstrate the immensity of God's love for us. He used the image of a mother hen. Jesus said, ***"O, Jerusalem, Jerusalem, . . .how often I have longed to gather your children together, as a hen gathers her chicks under her wings."*** I love the hymn "*Our God is Like an Eagle*" and the lines that say: ***"[o]ur God is not a*** *woman, our God is not a man; [o]ur God is both and neither, our God is I Who Am."*[15] *So, what is God like?* Well, on this first Sunday of Women's History Month, I want us to consider that *"God is like - A Mother's Love."*

What is God like? As I struggled with that question, I was reminded of the story of the little girl who was drawing a picture in her Sunday School class. The teacher asked, **"Who are you drawing a picture of?"** The little girl answered, **"God."** The teacher said, **"But no one knows what God looks like."** The little girl continued to draw her picture and responded, **"Well, they will in a few minutes."**

Well more than what God looks like, many of us want to know what is God like? We read our Bibles. We experience miracle after miracle in our lives. We have prayer after prayer answered, but still (probably because we cannot sit down and speak with God) we want to know more. The image from our gospel text may unnerve some folks and be a source of delight for others. If we take it seriously, it will broaden and deepen our understanding of who God is and how God works in our lives. The image offered is that God is *"like a hen gathering her chicks under her wings."*

When I think of a mother hen gathering her chicks under her wings, I am reminded of so many wonderful and powerful images of love and protection. I remember that when a mother hen leads her chicks, she walks in front of them, showing them the path to take. And even though she

---

[15]Bernier, Laurence G. *"Our God Is Like an Eagle."* Boston, 1974. Music composed by George James Webb (1803-1887), Public Domain, 1830, 1837.

is in front of them, she keeps a careful watch over every one of them, even the ones in the very back. If even the last little chick strays from the path, the mother hen quickly guides that little chick back in line. When the mother hen senses danger, she gathers the chicks under her wings and calms and quiets them until the danger passes. If the danger does not pass as quickly as the mother hen thinks it should pass, the mother hen is willing to sacrifice herself for the safety of her chicks.

This image of God as a mother hen brought back to me a memory from my childhood. I grew up in a small community called "Rock Run," in Southern Virginia, and there was a lake where lots of us kids went swimming in the summer. It was near the home of an old couple, affectionately known as Aunt Siney and Uncle Buster. I noticed an occurrence on that lake one day and the way Uncle Buster explained that occurrence broadened my childhood view of love and parental protection.

A mother duck, with her seven ducklings, was on the far end of the lake and I wanted to get a closer look at them. As I approached that part of the lake, the mother duck became immediately aware of my presence and gathered her little brood and hustled them together under her wings into the reeds and brushes that surrounded the edge of the lake. When I got really close to get a better look, the mother duck did something very odd. She started making all of this loud and awful noise, and then she just flew away, leaving all of the ducklings behind, alone. I thought *"What a coward!"* I hollered at her *"You stupid duck!"* You see, I thought she was a mother abandoning her young.

But Uncle Buster, who had been watching the whole thing, said, **"The mother duck knows what she's doing; she ain't stupid. Making all that noise and flying away is her way of protecting those little ducks."** I found out that day that the mother duck was offering herself as a decoy. She was making all that noise, and then flying away, not because she was a coward, but to attract my attention. She wanted me to notice her and follow her, away from her ducklings. She was willing to sacrifice herself in order to protect her offspring.

Now, maybe we can better understand the lament and the passion in Jesus' own voice found in our Gospel lesson today. It is the lament and passion of a mother who is worried about all of us--God's children.

Like a mother, Jesus sees the dangers of this world far more clearly than we do. Like a mother, Jesus knows we tend to overestimate our own knowledge, strength, and powers. Like little chicks, we often get out of line and stray from the path that God has set for us. We are prone to scattering on our own, leaving the protective wings of God's love and God's care, to seek our own excitement and adventure. Like a loving mother, Jesus chases after us, to nudge us back in line, to gather us under the wings of God's love, and to protect us. Like a loving mother, Jesus loves us so much that he was willing to sacrifice himself for us. Jesus does what His love compels Him to do. He pursues and protects His flock with a passion!

Now, I know that this feminine image of God will be disconcerting for some of you. Most of us have been raised with only a masculine image of God. However, in our gospel lesson today, we are given another image--one of a mother hen, with all her love and passion for her children, gathering them under her protective wings.

This image of God as a mother hen is as wonderful and as descriptive as any other image in the Bible in helping us to understand what God is like. I think it helps us to have this image of God as a loving mother. It helps us to understand how God longs for us--God's children. It helps us understand God's concern for our protection and God's willingness to sacrifice on our account. Maybe it takes this image of a mother's love to understand God's pain at our rejection of God's love.

Consider this thought: the thing that hurt Jesus the most was not the spear in His side, the iron nails in His hands, or the crown of thorns on His head. What hurt the most was the rejection by the very ones He had come to save.

So, in this image of a loving mother, we have a mirror of our relationship with God. On one hand, there is God's passionate effort to protect and save us. On the other hand, there is our persistent rebellion to God's power and our opposition to God's grace, as we seek to do our own thing and go our own way.

A real mother's love can be rejected but it cannot be stopped. I was one of the blessed people in this world because I actually had the chance to glimpse what unconditional love was like from my parents in the emotional security blanket they gave me and my siblings as we left to go out into the world on our own. They told us **"I don't care where you go and what you do, you're mine,**

I love you and you can always come home."[16] I have often said that I have never had to go home because I could not make it in life, but maybe one reason that I never had to go home is because I knew I had my parents' unconditional love and that I could go home if I needed to do so.

But I want to make it clear to you that unconditional love from my parents does not even come close to God's unconditional love for you and me. The Cross of Christ has become the symbol of outstretched arms that gather all of God's children, "**whosoever will**," into a community of love and grace. A real mother's love does not stop loving just because her love is not returned. Her love is not conditioned by the response of her child to it. Her love simply **IS**--period!

What a wonderful image of God! It shows us that God's love for us is so passionate that He is willing to protect us and gather us under His wings. It also shows us that God is willing to sacrifice His life, through Jesus Christ, for ours!

What is God like? **God is Like - A Mother's Love.** My hope is that God will continually come to us in new ways and in fresh images, so that our community can be moved and inspired to take risks to join in God's compassion for us--Her children.

Reverend Michael S. Piazza, the former Senior Pastor and Dean of the Cathedral of Hope in Dallas, Texas, and the current Senior Pastor of the Virginia-Highland Church in Atlanta, Georgia, penned the words to a little chorus that helps us with this feminine image of God. The words say:

---

[16] My parents, Jack and James Ella Reid Finney.

O tender Mother, hear our prayer,
As we children gather near
We offer you our wounded souls,
For your caress, can make us whole.[17]

---

[17]"*O Tender Mother*," written by Michael Piazza. Used with permission.

CHAPTER 6: GOD IS LIKE – A FORGIVING FATHER

A sermon using the following scriptures:

The Gospel Text: Luke 15:11-32

[11]Jesus [said]: "There was a man who had two sons. [12]The younger one said to his father, 'Father, give me my share of the estate.' So he divided his property between them. [13]Not long after that, the younger son got together all he had, set off for a distant country and there squandered his wealth in wild living. [14]After he had spent everything, there was a severe famine in that whole country, and he began to be in need. [15]So he went and hired himself out to a citizen of that country, who sent him to his fields to feed pigs. [16]He longed to fill his stomach with the pods that the pigs were eating, but no one gave him anything. [17]When he came to his senses, he said, 'How many of my father's hired men have food to spare, and here I am starving to death! [18]I will set out and go back to my father and say to him: Father, I have sinned against heaven and against you. [19]I am no longer worthy to be called your son; make me like one of your hired men.' [20]So he got up and went to his father. But while he was still a long way off, his father saw him and was filled with compassion for him; he ran to his son, threw his arms around him and kissed him. [21]The son said to him, 'Father, I have sinned against heaven and against you. I am no longer worthy to be called your son.' [22]But the father said to his servants, 'Quick! Bring the best robe and put it on him. Put a ring on his finger and sandals on his feet. [23]Bring the fattened calf and kill it. Let's have a feast and celebrate. [24]For this son of mine

was dead and is alive again; he was lost and is found.' So they began to celebrate.

25Meanwhile, the older son was in the field. When he came near the house, he heard music and dancing. 26So he called one of the servants and asked him what was going on. 27'Your brother has come,' he replied, 'and your father has killed the fattened calf because he has him back safe and sound.'

28The older brother became angry and refused to go in. So his father went out and pleaded with him. 29But he answered his father, 'Look! All these years I've been slaving for you and never disobeyed your orders. Yet you never gave me even a young goat so I could celebrate with my friends. 30But when this son of yours who has squandered your property with prostitutes comes home, you kill the fattened calf for him!'

31'My son,' the father said, 'you are always with me, and everything I have is yours. 32But we had to celebrate and be glad, because this brother of yours was dead and is alive again; he was lost and is found.' "

THE SERMON

Today is the fourth Sunday in our Lenten Journey for this church calendar year. Two weeks ago, on the first Sunday of Women's History Month, I talked about feminine images of God, because we need to stretch our minds and our concepts of what God is like. The sermon told us that ***"God is Like – A Mother's Love"*** and there was that wonderful imagery of Jesus in Luke's Gospel, lamenting over Jerusalem and saying, ***"how often I have longed to gather your children together, as a hen gathers her chicks*** *under her [protective] wings."* We saw how God loves us with an all-encompassing protective love.

In our sermon today, the image of God in the Gospel is found in the well-known story of **"The Prodigal Son."** So today, I want to talk about another wonderful image of God: **"God is Like – A Forgiving Father."**

How many of you have seen the movie or the play *"Sordid Lives?"* There is a stage production of it going on at TNT[18] over at the Dr. Pepper Center. It is a hilarious story about what initially appears to be a very dysfunctional family. Ty is handsome. Waddell is hot and the rest are just crazy. You know something is really wrong when Ruth Buzzi and Jane Hathaway are the sources of intimate fantasies! I strongly recommend you go see it.

If I had to write a review of the storyline of *"Sordid Lives"* it would go like this: *"The dialogue is funny. The voice tones are very serious. Every character lives his or her life on the edge of apprehension. When they meet with each other, their constant thought is "what have I done wrong, now?"*

The last line of that review would very much summarize how many of us feel about meeting God. We think we must be in trouble and ask ourselves *"what have I done wrong, now?"* Despite the fact that at Covenant we talk a lot about how God loves us, I get the distinct impression that many of us feel that God just tolerates us. Many of us feel that, because of our *"Sordid Lives"* and because of

---

[18] TNT is the "Terrific New Theatre" in Birmingham, Alabama.

who we really are, God would just love to get His hands on us!!

Now some of us would not go that far. We would say, *"Oh, I know that God loves me, but I must confess that God probably does not like me too much."* Well, if you think God is "put out" with you because of your *"Sordid Life"* then today's Gospel lesson reveals for you a real and wonderful truth: **"God is Like – A Forgiving Father."**

Every time I read the parable of the prodigal son, I am convinced of two things: First, the parable of the prodigal son goes a long way toward answering the question, what is God like? Second, this parable is aimed at anyone who is troubled and uncertain about how God feels about him or her.

Most of us know the story. An apparently wealthy man has two sons. The oldest son stays home and helps the father in the family business, but the youngest son, who becomes known as the prodigal son, asks for his share of what would be his inheritance and goes off to the far country and squanders it all. When he is completely broke, he has to find a job. The prodigal son finally ends up doing one of the most degrading things a Jewish person could think of doing -- feeding pigs. His life has become a sordid life. Jesus really gives us a horrifying image of what the prodigal son's life has become. The reason Jesus paints such a horrific picture of this young man's life is because Jesus is trying to make us understand the greatness of God and the enormity of God's love for us.

The prodigal son's life has become so "messed up" that there was nothing left in him that could motivate the father to love him. If the father still loves him now, then it is only because that is just the nature of the father.

The prodigal son finally realizes the futility of his life and his choices. Then he thought of his father and how even his father's servants live more comfortably than he is living; so, the prodigal son decides to return home. An important thing to notice about this story, as recorded in Luke's Gospel, is that there is no mention of the prodigal son cleaning himself up first. There is no mention of him getting his life together first. All we are told is that he comes to his senses. As far as we know, the prodigal son returned home wearing the same old dirty rags he wore when he fed the pigs.

The picture carefully created by Jesus shows the father with open arms welcoming his son back home. It shows a father extending unconditional love to a son who had fled from the good home life that the father had created for him and had squandered all the inheritance that the father had given to him. But, this unconditional love is Jesus' point. This story of the prodigal son is about how much God loves us.

The story of the prodigal son demonstrates five great truths about God's love, which I want us to consider. I do not claim that these are the only truths about God's love, or even the only truths about God's love found in the story. However, I find these five truths to be crucially important to our understanding and appreciation of God's love for us.

First, the story of the prodigal son tells us that God's love has no limits.

If there was a breaking point where the father had been pushed too far, certainly this young man should have found that breaking point. The prodigal son crossed every line in the sand that the father could have drawn. The prodigal son refused to help with the family business. He demanded his inheritance, even before the father died. He took his money and went to a far country, away from his father's home, and he squandered all of the money. Some of us have done exactly the same thing with our *"Sordid Lives."* But the point is clear. From the father's perspective, however, there is no condemnation. He does not greet his son by saying, *"Well, I never thought I'd see you again!"* Neither does he say, *"Go get help from the people you spent your money on."* No, the father greets the son with open arms!

Listen carefully, I do not care what you have done; you have not stretched yourself beyond the limits of God's love. God's love for you knows no limits.

Second, the story tells us that God's love is a patient love.

We do not know how long this son had been gone. It was long enough for him to apparently go through a whole lot of money, but Jesus did not give us a specific time frame. Yet, we get the strong impression that the father never stopped looking down the road for his son's return. When the prodigal son finally returns we are told that the father sees him from a long distance. The father sees him because the father was constantly watching for him and hoping for his return home.

The point is clear: **God is Like – A Forgiving Father**, whose love is a patient love. God patiently waits for us, even when we have turned aside or run away from Him. God does not sit and scheme about what God is going to do, if and when we come back. God's desire is not revenge; revenge does not promote love. God loves us and desires a restoration for each of us who has gone astray. In I Corinthians 13:4, the Apostle Paul talks about love. The first two attributes Paul lists are that *"Love is patient [and] . . . kind!"*

Third, this story shows that God's love is eager.

Jesus made this point clear in the parable. When the father saw his youngest son coming from a far distance, the father ran and embraced and kissed his son. In first century Palestine, no one who had dignity would be seen running in public. But when the father sees his son, he forgets about the impression he might make on other people. He is overwhelmed with joy because of his son's return. It is more important to the father to have his youngest son safely back into his home than to worry about the impression he might make on his neighbors!

This notion of God the Father running must have stunned the Pharisees who were listening to Jesus. *How could this Jesus be so brazen in portraying God running and eagerly throwing his arms around a sinner?* That image is not how they pictured God. Instead, they saw God only as the chastiser of sinners, in much the same way as God is viewed by many of the "Christians" of today.

The truth is that God is most eager to reestablish a relationship with you after you have sinned. Just like the forgiving father in this parable, God is eagerly waiting for us to return home to God's love. Moreover, God's love is extravagant. The Apostle Paul says *"[God] who did not spare his own Son, but gave [Christ] up for us all – how will [God] not also, with [Christ], graciously give us all things?"[19]* God's love is eager!

Fourth, the story teaches that God's focus is on the sinner, not the sin.

Upon returning, the son immediately begins to recite his prepared speech: *"Father, I have sinned against heaven and against you. I am no longer worthy to be called your son."* The son's focus, like ours, was on his *"Sordid Life"* and his unworthiness. In essence, he was begging for mercy. He knew what he deserved and he was saying: *"I am willing to take what is coming to me."*

But the focus of the father is very different. The father seems to ignore his son's speech. He does not shout at the son; instead, he shouts orders to his servant: *Quick! Bring the best robe and put it on him. Put a ring on his finger and sandals on his feet. Bring the fattened calf and kill it. Let's have a feast and celebrate. For this son of mine was dead and is alive again; he was lost and is found.'"* The father's focus is on his son.

---

[19] Romans 8:32.

This story tells you that your sin has already been dealt with by God. It is no longer the focus of God. You are God's focus. If you need to confess something, do it today, so that you can begin to realize that you are the focus of God's attention. That sin, event, or thing that keeps haunting you and making you feel depressed, miserable, and restless is no longer a wall between you and your relationship with God. When you repent and return home to God's fellowship and love, what you have done and how long you have done it is no longer a consideration. As far as we know, in the story of the prodigal son, the father never even asked his son how he wasted all that money. That issue did not matter. What mattered was that his son was back home. **God is Like – A Forgiving Father**. God focuses on you and not what you have done.

Fifth, and finally, the story demonstrates that God's love is a joyful love.

The older brother, who had remained home and helped his father in the family business, is not as eager as the father to see the return of his younger brother. When he sees the royal treatment the younger brother is getting, the older brother begins to complain about what seems to be a free ride. The older brother is angry and he lets Daddy know about his feelings. But the father is not persuaded by the older son's complaints. The father answers the older son this way: **"But we had to celebrate and be glad, because this brother of yours was dead and is alive again; he was lost and is found."**

It is hard for some of us to relate to the father's overwhelming joy because joy is not the response that we have when someone has hurt us. Under similar circumstances, we might try our very best to act civilized, but joy is not what we would be feeling towards our family member who acted like the prodigal son. But, the difference between the way we would probably respond and the way the father responds is another thing that makes the father's love so amazing in this story. The father did not allow his own hurt, which was real, to get in the way of the son's needs, which were also real. Jesus said, ***"[t]hey began to celebrate."*** That verse sounds like a pretty joyful return to me. ***"'[B]ut this is a wonderful time, and we had to celebrate. This brother of yours was dead, and he's alive! He was lost, and he's found!'"*** [20]

You may be looking back over your *"Sordid Life"* and thinking that today's message is just too good to be true! You may think you are far from God's unconditional love. If so, then perhaps you need to change your attitude about God and come home to five important facts about God's love:

1) God's love for you has no limits.
1) God's love for you is a patient love.
2) God's love for you is an eager love.
3) God's love for you focuses on you, and not what you have done.
4) God's love for you is a joyful love.

It does not matter what you have done in the past; you too can come home to God's love. That is the nature of God.

---

[20] Luke 15:32 as quoted from *The Message: The Bible in Contemporary Language.* Trans. Eugene H. Peterson. Colorado: NavPress Publishing Group, 2002.

There is nothing too big or too hard for God's love to cover or forgive. There is nothing too bad or too old for God's forgiveness. **God is Like – A Forgiving Father.**

CHAPTER 7: <u>CHRIST THE KING: WHAT I DID FOR LOVE!</u>

A sermon using the following scriptures:

The Epistle Text: Colossians 1:15-20

[15] *He is the image of the invisible God, the firstborn over all creation.* [16] *For by him all things were created: things in heaven and on earth, visible and invisible, whether thrones or powers or rulers or authorities; all things were created by him and for him.* [17] *He is before all things, and in him all things hold together.* [18] *And he is the head of the body, the church; he is the beginning and the firstborn from among the dead, so that in everything he might have the supremacy.* [19] *For God was pleased to have all his fullness dwell in him,* [20] *and through him to reconcile to himself all things, whether things on earth or things in heaven, by making peace through his blood, shed on the cross.*

The Gospel Text: Luke 23:32-43

[32] *Two other men, both criminals, were also led out with [Jesus] to be executed.* [33] *When they came to the place called the Skull, there they crucified him, along with the criminals – one on his right, the other on his left.* [34] *Jesus said, "Father, forgive them, for they do not know what they are doing." And they divided up his clothes by casting lots.* [35] *The people stood watching, and the rulers even sneered at him. They said, "He saved others; let him save himself if he is the Christ of God, the Chosen One."* [36] *The soldiers also came up and mocked him. They offered him wine vinegar* [37] *and said, "If you are the king of the Jews, save yourself."* [38] *There was a written notice above him, which read: THIS IS THE KING OF THE JEWS.* [39] *One of the*

criminals who hung there hurled insults at him: "Aren't you the Christ? Save yourself and us!" [40]*But the other criminal rebuked him. "Don't you fear God," he said, "since you are under the same sentence?* [41]*We are punished justly, for we are getting what our deeds deserved. But this man has done nothing wrong."* [42]*Then he said, "Jesus, remember me when you come into your kingdom."* [43]*Jesus answered him, "I tell you the truth, today you will be with me in paradise."*

THE SERMON

Today is the last Sunday of the liturgical church calendar year. So, today we celebrate **"Christ the King Sunday!"** This Sunday is the day on which we remind ourselves of the sovereign reign of Christ as King of Kings and Lord of Lords!!

Someone once asked a little girl to tell them who Jesus was and she responded by saying that Jesus was *"God with skin."* While most of us can appreciate the simplicity and humor of the little girl's answer, we also recognize the truth contained within that answer. In our Epistle reading for today, the Apostle Paul, in describing Jesus, says, *"He is the image of the invisible God . . ."* *"And He is the head of the body, the church . . . so that in everything He might have the supremacy."*

Most of us have already started the frantic Christmas shopping, the fighting for bargains, and the making of the lists and checking them twice. However, before we go any further, let us stop today to remember *"Christ the King" and "What He Did for Love."*

Years ago, when I lived in Memphis, Tennessee, I was part of a benefit show at a place called *"George's Crisco Disco & Drag Bar."* The benefit show was staged to raise funds for *The Memphis Coalition*, one of the first prominent gay rights organizations in Memphis. There were many wonderful and creative acts that night; however, the act that brought down the house was performed by a drag queen who limped out on stage, battered, bruised, and scarred. She had a crutch, a cane, and casts that covered one leg, one arm, and part of the other arm. She stood there, and in her own voice, sang *a cappella*, **"Kiss today goodbye, and point me t'ward tomorrow, We did what we had to do. Won't forget, can't regret what I did for love."**[21]

As I remember that scene and the song today, I am reminded that this scene depicts exactly what Jesus Christ is saying to us on this Christ the King Sunday. When Jesus remembers the thirty lashes, the nails that scarred his hands and feet, and the scars left from the piercing of his sides -- when Jesus remembers the pain and suffering that he endured for our sins, Jesus still says **"Won't forget, can't regret, what I did for love."**

It is somewhat ironic that on the Sunday before we begin our Advent celebration of Christ's birth, we are confronted in the lectionary gospel with the image of Jesus dying on the cross. Yet the two are inseparable – Christmas and the Cross. It is impossible to appreciate the events of Bethlehem, except in the light of the events of Golgotha,

---

[21] Hamlisch, Marvin (Music) and Edward Kleban (Lyrics). "What I Did For Love." *A Chorus Line*. Edward Kleban and Famous Music LLC, 1975.

because without the Christmas story, there is no Cross and, without the Cross, we would never understand **"What Jesus did for love!"** So on this Christ the King Sunday, let's explore why Jesus did what He did for love, by looking at three simple, but important points:

FIRST, JESUS DIED FOR US BECAUSE GOD LOVES US.

Dr. Fred B. Craddock, renowned minister and Bandy Professor of Teaching and New Testament (Emeritus) at the Candler School of Theology, tells a story[22] about a family taking a Sunday afternoon drive, when suddenly the children began shouting, **"Stop the car! There is a kitten in the road."** Dad kept driving, but the children refused to quiet down. Dad tried to reason with them: The kitten was probably someone's pet. It might have a disease, and besides, we already have too many pets, as it is. All of his wise and adult reasoning fell on deaf ears. So finally, Dad drove back, got out of the car, and reached down to pick up the scrawny little kitten. Just as he was about to pick up the kitten, the ungrateful little thing scratched him! Dad's natural instinct was to leave the kitten in the road, but being a compassionate man (and knowing what his children would think) Dad packed the kitten into the car and took it home. The family took the kitten to a veterinarian, got its shots, made a bed for it, fed it, petted it, fussed all over it, and generally did everything one normally does with a new pet. Soon, the kitten was purring and rubbing on family

---

[22] Craddock, Fred B. *Craddock Stories.* Ed. Mike Graves and Richard F. Ward. St. Louis: Chalice Press, 2001, pp. 24-25.

members, especially Dad. In fact, it seemed that Dad had become the kitten's favorite family member!

Dad looked at the scars on his hand left by a frightened and seemingly ungrateful kitten, just a few weeks ago. Then he looked at the comfortable, well-fed kitten rubbing against his leg. *Had the father become more worthy of the kitten's love?* No. His intentions towards the kitten had always been to do it good, not harm. But something had happened to the kitten that made it feel secure, loved, and accepted.

How often does God try to bless us and we respond by scratching God's hand? What Christ wants us to understand today is **"what he did for love."** Maybe someone told you that you were not worthy of God's love. Maybe someone does not accept you for who you are. But you should always know that God's intentions toward you have always been to make you feel secure, loved, and accepted. Jesus looks at the scars on His hand and He wants you to know **"what he did for love."** The hand that reached down to bless your life--the hand that initially belonged to that precious babe in the manger--is now covered with the bruises, the wounds, and the scratches from the Cross. *Why did Jesus come?* **He came because God loves us. Our understanding of both the manger and the cross is that Jesus was born and Jesus died for no other reason than -** *God loves us.*

SECOND, JESUS DID IT BECAUSE GOD REFUSES TO LET GO OF US.

In John 10:27-29, Jesus emphasizes this point. He is talking about you and me as believers in Christ and He says: *"My sheep listen to my voice. . . . I give them eternal life, and they shall never perish; no one can snatch them out of my hand. My Father, who has given them to me, is greater than all; no one can snatch them out of my Father's hand."* I often add my own postscript to that verse: And you cannot jump out either. Why? **God refuses to let go of us**.

There is a wonderful story on the Internet that helps better illustrate this image of God's love.[23] A little boy in Florida lay in a hospital bed, his body riddled with cuts and bruises. He had been swimming in a local lake, when an alligator surfaced a few feet away. The boy's Mom spotted the alligator first. She ran for the lake and grabbed hold of her son's arms just as the alligator, with his powerful jaws, caught the meaty part of the boy's leg. As you might expect, the Mom won that crucial tug-of-war. During a hospital visit, the boy's little friend stared in gruesome fascination at the stitches in his friend's leg, but the injured little boy was more proud of the injuries to his arms. He

---

[23] Combs, Kelly. "Alligator Scars." *Chatty Kelly - Chatting About God's Love – Sometimes Teaching, Always Learning.* 21 Sept 2009.
< http://www.chattykelly.com/2009/09/alligator-scars.html.> and "Scars of Life." *PreparingForEternity.com – Bringing God's Last Day Message of Love to the World!*
<http://www.preparingforeternity.com/scars.htm. >
Although the two stories differ as to whether it was the mother or father who saved the child, the point about the strength of a parent's love is abundantly clear.

held out his skinny arms covered with scratches and bruises and proudly said, **"These marks were made by my Mom, because she refused to let go."**

In a song called *"Mercy Said No,"* that has been recorded by Cece Winans, the chorus has these words:

> Mercy said no
> I'm not gonna let you go
> I'm not gonna let you slip away
> You don't have to be afraid
> Mercy said no
>
> . . .
>
> Life and death stood face to face
> Darkness tried to steal my heart away
> Thank you Jesus
> Mercy said no.[24]

On this Christ the King Sunday, if you are wondering why Jesus did **what He did for love, know that He did it because *"Mercy said, No!,"* and God refuses to let go of us!**

---

[24] Long, Greg, Don Koch and Dave Clark. "Mercy Said No." Word Music, LLC/Inferataste Music/Curlin Music/DaySpring Music, LLC/Definitive Music/First Verse Music, 1998. Perf. CeCe Winans. *Throne Room*, 2003.

THIRD, JESUS DID IT BECAUSE GOD SEES SOMETHING IN US.

That thought is an awesome one, and it shows us that God sees something in us worth saving. Covenant is a great church; I am so blessed to be a part of it. Before the staff and Board meetings, we always have a time of sharing and praying together. I often say to them as I did with the Board last Tuesday, sometimes I have to pinch myself to see if it is true that God allows me to pastor this great church. You see, I never saw myself as the pastor of this church, but God did.

Last Sunday in the children's moment one of our deacons made a statement that he often says about me and himself. He said, *"If God can use our Pastor, or me, then God can use anybody."* Without a doubt, our deacon is right this time! That statement is our deacon's way of saying that God sees something in each of us. The Apostle Peter said, in Acts 10:34-35, *"**I now realize how true it is that God does not show favoritism, but accepts everyone. . .**"* That acceptance is what our deacon is talking about when he makes his statement. I stand before you and tell you today that with all my imperfections, with all of our deacon's imperfections, with all your imperfections, and all of our sins as well, **God loves us because God sees something in each of us worth saving.**

Did you notice the last part of the gospel story today? As Jesus hangs on a cross between two thieves, one of them hurls insults at him. *"**Aren't you the Christ? Save yourself and us!**" But the other [thief] rebuked him. "Don't you fear God, since you are under the same* *sentence? We are punished justly, for we are getting what our deeds deserve. But this man has done nothing wrong.* Then he said, *"Jesus, remember me when You come into Your kingdom."* Jesus saw something in that second thief and answered him and said, *"I tell you the truth, today you will be with me in paradise."* Jesus is still saying to us today —*"What I did for love was to die for you. You, who believe in me, will be with me in paradise."*

So, we come to this Christ the King Sunday confessing that without God's love and mercy, we have no hope. But as the Apostle Paul said, *"For God was pleased to have all His fullness dwell in [Christ], and through [Christ] to reconcile to [God's] self all things . . . by making peace through [Christ's] blood, shed on the cross.* Yes, what Jesus did for love was simply to die for us! **Jesus died for us because**

1) **God loves us;**
2) **God refuses to let go of us; and**
3) **God sees something in us worth saving.**

So on this Christ the King Sunday, **we have abundant hope about life, about death, and about life beyond death**. Jesus proclaims to us on this Christ the King Sunday, **"What I did for love!"**

PART III:
LIFE AS A CHRISTIAN

"Life is a journey not a destination." (Unknown)
*"I come that you might have life and have it more
abundantly."* John 10:10

In Part II, the sermons were designed to help people come
to faith in Christ by understanding, knowing and believing
in God's love for them. *After coming to faith, then what?*
In Part III, the sermons take us--as followers of Christ--
beyond our initial faith of trusting and believing in God's
love to the challenging task of living *"Life as a Christian."*
The sermons in this section help us to realize that believing
in God's love is only the first step because *"the Christian
Life is a journey, not a destination."* On our Christian
journey, we need to receive regular spiritual nourishment
through worship; we need to see our faith in action through
our service; and we need to find encouragement in God's
word through scripture study in order to live out our faith
victoriously. These sermons assist us in overcoming the
adversities of life and living the promise of abundant life
that Jesus speaks of in John 10:10.

CHAPTER 8:
THE HEALING POWER
OF FORGIVENESS

A sermon using the following scriptures:

The Epistle Text: Romans 14:1, 9-14

[1]Accept him whose faith is weak, without passing judgment on disputable matters.

[9]For this very reason, Christ died and returned to life so that he might be the Lord of both the dead and the living. [10]You, then, why do you judge your brother? Or why do you look down on your brother? For we will all stand before God's judgment seat. [11]It is written: "'As surely as I live,' says the Lord, 'every knee will bow before me; every tongue will confess to God.'" [12]So then, each of us will give an account of himself to God. [13]Therefore let us stop passing judgment on one another. Instead, make up your mind not to put any stumbling block or obstacle in your brother's way. [14]As one who is in the Lord Jesus, I am fully convinced that no food is unclean in itself. But if anyone regards something as unclean, then for him it is unclean.

The Gospel Text: Matthew 18:21-35

[21]Then Peter came to Jesus and asked, "Lord, how many times shall I forgive my brother when he sins against me? Up to seven times?" [22]Jesus answered, "I tell you, not seven times, but seventy-seven times.

[23]"Therefore, the kingdom of heaven is like a king who wanted to settle accounts with his servants. [24]As he began the settlement, a man who owed him ten thousand talents was brought to him. [25]Since he was not able to pay, the

master ordered that he and his wife and his children and all that he had be sold to repay the debt.

26 *"The servant fell on his knees before him. 'Be patient with me,' he begged, 'and I will pay back everything.'* 27 *The servant's master took pity on him, canceled the debt and let him go.*

28 *"But when that servant went out, he found one of his fellow servants who owed him a hundred denarii. He grabbed him and began to choke him. 'Pay back what you owe me!' he demanded.*

29 *"His fellow servant fell to his knees and begged him, 'Be patient with me, and I will pay you back.'* 30 *"But he refused. Instead, he went off and had the man thrown into prison until he could pay the debt.* 31 *When the other servants saw what had happened, they were greatly distressed and went and told their master everything that had happened.*

32 *"Then the master called the servant in. 'You wicked servant,' he said, 'I canceled all that debt of yours because you begged me to.* 33 *Shouldn't you have had mercy on your fellow servant just as I had on you?'* 34 *In anger his master turned him over to the jailers to be tortured, until he should pay back all he owed.*

35 *"This is how my heavenly Father will treat each of you unless you forgive your brother from your heart."*

THE SERMON

The gospel lesson from Matthew is very familiar to most of us. Peter's question to Jesus was a very sincere one. Prominent rabbis of that day were teaching that one should forgive his brother three times. So one day Peter asked Jesus, *"Lord, how many times shall I forgive my brother when he sins against me? Up to seven times?" Jesus answered, "I tell you, not seven times, but seventy-seven times."*

Forgiveness is a huge problem in our lives today. For many of us there have been persons who have really hurt and wronged us. Much of the trauma we are going through today is because we have not been able to let go of our anger, resentment, and sometimes, even hatred caused by what others have done to us in the past. Many of us hang on to that anger, resentment, and hatred, long after the person who has wronged us has forgotten about what they did or, in some cases, long after that person who has wronged us has died. Psychologists and psychiatrists tell us that harboring anger, resentment, and hatred hurts us more than it hurts the person or persons against whom we are holding these emotions. For our own benefit, we must learn how to forgive those who we believe have wronged us. Therefore, let us take time and consider **"The Healing Power of Forgiveness."**

In today's gospel text, which is taken from *The Holy Bible, New International Version*®, Jesus says we should forgive a person seventy-seven times when that person wrongs us. In the King James Version (KJV), Jesus says we must forgive seventy times seven, which is 490 times,[25] or, in other words, a countless number of times. Jesus is saying that if you want to find healing, peace, and wholeness, you need to become familiar with *The Healing Power of Forgiveness.* Jesus teaches us not to keep track, not to hold onto anger and resentment. Jesus wants us to learn to

---

[25] Matthew 18:22 (KJV); see also, Luke 17:4.

forgive because forgiveness is essential to our mental, emotional, and spiritual wellbeing.

For some of us, it is difficult to forgive because our pain is so deep! It may have been a teacher, a parent, a friend, a spouse, or even a child, but somewhere along the way someone hurt us deeply and we can still feel that pain. Some of you can see that person's face (even as I speak) and the pain is so intense that it is easier to just cut that person out of your life than to forgive them.

I was in Virginia last weekend where I had the privilege to preach the memorial service for our family's annual reunion. The service was held at Mt. Olive East Christian Church, my grandparents' home church. I was so glad to see a certain cousin there this year because he had not been to the family reunion in several years, even though he lives right there in the community where the reunion is held. *Why had he not been there?* He had stayed away because he had been harboring resentment and anger against some of the other family members. We were all so very happy to see him and to have him be a part of our celebrations again, and he appeared to be genuinely glad that he was once more in our midst. I was glad to see that forgiveness had finally worked its way into his heart and into the hearts of our other family members.

As glad as I was to see him, I was struck by the lesson to be learned from that situation. For, you see, although his resentment and anger against some other family members had kept him from attending our family reunions, neither his feelings nor his absence had stopped even one reunion from being held. The rest of us, including the family members against whom his resentment and anger were directed, continued to have a wonderful time and great family reunions, even in his absence. Yes, we missed him and we prayed for him, but we enjoyed ourselves. When he chose to cut the family out of his life, rather than to forgive the few family members he felt had wronged him, my cousin was the one who lost out on the great joy and fun of being surrounded by hundreds of other loving cousins!

We must be very diligent about forgiveness. Our inability to forgive can have devastating personal effects on us. It can weaken our relationship with our family and friends, weaken our relationship with God, poison our memory about what actually happened, shorten our lives due to the stress of carrying such a burden, and even affect our own feelings of self-worth. So how do we discover **"The Healing Power of Forgiveness?"**

First, we must recognize that forgiveness is a gift from God.

Forgiveness is a wonderful gift. We have been forgiven by God and so we are able to forgive others. Jesus followed his answer to Peter with a parable that presents an excellent example for us all. Jesus told of a certain man who owed the king 10,000 talents, about 15 years of a laborer's wages in that day. The man was unable to pay his debt to the king, so the king ordered that the man, his wife, children, and all that he owned be sold to pay the debt. The man fell upon his knees and begged for mercy and patience, and promised to repay everything he owed. The king had great mercy on the man and forgave his debt.

This same man had a fellow servant who owed him 100 denarii, about one day's wage. When he saw his fellow servant, he grabbed him and began to choke him, and demanded repayment of all the money his fellow servant owed to him. The fellow servant fell to his knees and begged for patience, and promised that all the money would be repaid; however, the first servant, whose enormous debt had been forgiven by the king, could not forgive the tiny debt owed him by a fellow servant. He had his fellow servant thrown into jail until he could pay the debt.

The contrast between the actions of the king and his servant is striking. The king was able to forgive an enormous debt, while the servant was unwilling to forgive a small debt owed by a fellow servant. But, the story does not end here. When the king found out what the servant had done to his fellow servant, he became angry and turned the servant who owed to him the great sum of money over to the jailers to be tortured until he could pay back all he owed. Then Jesus told us the point of the parable. Jesus said **"[t]his is how my heavenly Father will treat each of you unless you forgive your brother from your heart."**

Of course Jesus is not simply telling an interesting story about some mythical man; Jesus is teaching you and me about forgiveness. We have all sinned; we have all done wrong; we have all been disobedient. Yet, we have been forgiven by a merciful and loving God. Remember our processional hymn, *"Great is Thy Faithfulness?"* The last verse of this beautiful hymn eloquently describes **"The Healing Power of Forgiveness."** The hymn writer wrote,

Pardon for sin and a peace that endureth
Thine own dear presence to cheer and to
guide;
Strength for today and bright hope for
tomorrow,
Blessings all mine, with ten thousand
beside![26]

That "peace that endureth" is **"The Healing Power of Forgiveness."** We forgive others because of the priceless, enormous gift of forgiveness that we have received from God. If we can come to recognize just how much God has forgiven us, that knowledge can be a powerful antidote to our feelings of resentment over wrongdoing by others. Additionally, Jesus has told us that, unless we forgive our brother or our sister from the heart, our heavenly Father does not forgive us. We discover **"The Healing Power of Forgiveness"** because we remember that God has forgiven us, so we are able to forgive others.

Second, we need to recognize that forgiveness is the most powerful witness we have of grace in our lives.

Sometime ago, I had a talk with the mother of our church, Mama Dorothy, and she shared with me some awful things a person had done to her. The things that this person had done had hurt her so badly that it kept eating at her spiritual and mental well-being. The more Mama Dorothy thought about it, the more it hurt; yet, this other person seemed unbothered about anything. Mama Dorothy said that she

---

[26] Chisholm, Thomas O. (1866-1960)(Words) and William M. Runyan (1870-1957)(Music). "Great is Thy Faithfulness." Hope Publishing Company, 1923, 1951.

had a choice whether to forgive that person or let what that person had done continue to eat at her and vex her for the rest of her life. She chose to forgive the person, and you know what, Mama Dorothy's life became better. Mama Dorothy's forgiveness is a powerful witness of God's grace in her life.

For some of us, though, we are nursing a grudge that has become a deep spiritual problem. It weakens our witness to Christ's presence in our lives and it damages us personally. I have said it several times before: *resentment hurts you more than the other person. It is like drinking poison and hoping the other person dies.* We need to follow Mama Dorothy's example and recognize that forgiveness is a gift from God to be passed on to others, and that giving forgiveness is the most powerful witness we have to the reality of God's grace in our own lives. It is **"The Healing Power of Forgiveness."**

Third, and finally, we need to recognize that forgiveness is a positive activity necessary to the healing and wholeness of our own hearts.

Forgiveness is not passive resignation to a bad situation. Forgiveness does not mean we shrug our shoulders and say, "Well, there is nothing else to do, so I might as well forgive." There is no healing or wholeness in that kind of forgiveness.

Forgiveness is a positive, joyful activity in which we learn to change from seeing ourselves as victims and start seeing ourselves as victors. Forgiveness allows us to move from weakness to strength, from inadequacy to self-affirmation, from pain to peace. The **"Healing Power of Forgiveness"** allows us to experience within our own lives the power and the presence of Christ.

Do you need to discover "The Healing Power of Forgiveness?" Is there someone you need to forgive? Maybe it was an unfaithful spouse, an overbearing parent, a friend who stabbed you in the back, or an employer who took advantage of you. Maybe it was that bully who made every day of school a living hell. Maybe it is that family member who makes it impossible for you to spend peaceful time with the rest of the family. The pain of that hurt is deep; the pain of that hurt is real. But, you do not have to continue to carry this pain. You do not have to continue to give someone else so much control over your life, over your well-being. You can claim the awesome **"Healing Power of Forgiveness"** that Jesus offers us.

We claim the **"Healing Power of Forgiveness"** by recognizing that forgiveness is a precious gift from God, beneficial to us in so many ways.

- God has forgiven us for our transgressions; therefore, we must forgive the people who have wronged us.
- Forgiveness is a powerful witness to God's grace in our lives. When we fail to forgive, it weakens our witness to God in our lives and causes us hurt, pain, and sorrow. In some cases, we become physically ill because of the stress of holding on to past wrongs that people have done to us.
- Forgiveness is a positive activity necessary for the healing and wholeness of our own hearts. We are

the greatest beneficiaries of our ability to forgive others. We are the ones who claim the greatest victory when we forgive. No longer do we allow another person to have control over us by what he or she has said or done. We release the resentment, pain, hurt, and anger and, in doing so, we are able to get closer to the loving and healing power of God.

Today, let us all start claiming the awesome **"Healing Power of Forgiveness."**

CHAPTER 9:
THE AWESOME POWER OF JOY

A sermon using the following scriptures:

The Epistle Text: I Thessalonians 5:16-18 and 23-24
[16]Be joyful always; [17]pray continually; [18]give thanks in all circumstances, for this is God's will for you in Christ Jesus. [23]May God himself, the God of peace, sanctify you through and through. May your whole spirit, soul and body be kept blameless at the coming of our Lord Jesus Christ. [24]The one who calls you is faithful and he will do it.

The Gospel Text: John 1:6-8 and 23-27
[6]There came a man who was sent from God; his name was John. [7]He came as a witness to testify concerning that light, so that through him all men might believe.
[8]He himself was not the light; he came only as a witness to the light.
[23]John replied in the words of Isaiah the prophet, "I am the voice of one calling in the desert, 'Make straight the way for the Lord.'" [24]Now some Pharisees who had been sent [25]questioned him, "Why then do you baptize if you are not the Christ, nor Elijah, nor the Prophet?"
[26]"I baptize with water," John replied, "but among you stands one you do not know. [27]He is the one who comes after me, the thongs of whose sandals I am not worthy to untie."

THE SERMON

Today is the third Sunday of Advent and the theme for today is "Joy." The themes for the three Sundays of

Advent are peace, love and joy. These three things also happen to be the first three aspects of the *"fruit of the spirit."*[27] Each one is vital to our spiritual health as we prepare in Advent for Christmas. Today, let's look at **"The Awesome Power of Joy."**

"The Awesome Power of Joy" -- All of us know what it is like to get that "Special" Christmas Gift that leaves us speechless. Well, in preparing this sermon, I found a few thoughts that you might express if you find yourself with such a gift this year:

> **"Oh No! I really don't deserve this."**
> **"I love it – but I fear the jealousy it will inspire."**
> **"If the dog buries it, I'm going to be furious!"**
> **"Oh, and to think I got this the year when I vowed to give all my gifts to Charity."**
> *(And my personal favorite)* **"Gosh, I hope this never catches fire. But it is fire season though. And there are a lot of unexplained fires."**

I hope those little quips made you laugh or at least smile. Laughter is great and doctors tell us that it is good for us. It is also a sign of happiness. But if you laughed or smiled, it is because the impetus for that laughter was an outside source (*me telling you those joke lines*).

Here is my point: **Do not confuse happiness with joy.** Happiness is based on outside influences. If things are going well, we are happy; if not, then we are not happy. But joy is an inside job and it is based on *"the fruit of the*

---

[27] Galatians 5:22.

spirit" in our lives. In Christ, we can have joy no matter how bad or distasteful our circumstances. *So, the question is: How do we experience* **"The Awesome Power of Joy?"**

The Epistle lesson for today from I Thessalonians instructs us to **"Be JOYFUL always . . . give thanks in all circumstances."** *How is that possible?* Well, I am convinced that it is possible. Every one of us can experience **"The Awesome Power of Joy"** if we will accept one principle. That principle is this: ***What we believe is more important than what we have or who we are.*** The most important matter in your life is not what is happening **TO** you, but what is happening **IN** you. I want to share with you four ways that what is happening in you either prevents you from experiencing or allows you to experience **"The Awesome Power of Joy."**

"The Awesome Power of Joy" is affected by what you believe about yourself.

The lives of many people in our community have been crippled by the negative things that society and churches have caused them to believe about themselves. When all they have been taught is that they are not good enough, that they are abominations to God, or that they cannot be a part of God's family as they are . . . then many people develop negative and distorted self images. These distorted self images destroy their self esteem and lead them to do destructive things to themselves.

I can tell you a million times that God loves you, but it will not help you one bit unless you truly begin to believe it.

Accordingly, my prayer for you is that the Holy Spirit will take my words and make them come alive in you.

What you believe about yourself is more important than your talent, your skin color, your gender, your sexual orientation, your I.Q., or even your social status. If you want to experience **"The Awesome Power of Joy,"** then there is a way to do it: Start believing that you are a unique creation of God, and that God loves God's creation--YOU. If you can come to believe that God loves you and created you to be a winner in life, you will be a blessing to yourself and to others. Experiencing **"The Awesome Power of Joy"** begins with what you believe about yourself.

"The Awesome Power of Joy" is affected by what you believe about your purpose for living.

One thing that seems to be very hard for many in our community to believe is that God has a purpose for their lives. When you do not believe that you are special to God, it is almost impossible to believe that God has a purpose for your living. These two beliefs must work together before you can begin to experience **"The Awesome Power of Joy."** Advent is a time of preparing for the coming of the Christ Child. Perhaps this year, it is the time we each start preparing for the coming of the Christ by believing in God's purpose for our living.

No matter the circumstances of your birth, you are NOT an accident to God. Maybe the reason Jesus was born in the midst of troubling circumstances (*to an unwed peasant teenage girl in Palestine*) was because God knew that most of us would also start life with difficult hurdles to face.

The example of Jesus is that He believed in His purpose for living. *Do you know yours? Better yet, if you do know it, do you believe in your purpose for living?*

Let me share with you one of my favorite verses from the Bible that illustrates what I am saying. In Jeremiah 29:11, God says to Jeremiah, and to us today as well, ***"For I know the plans I have for you . . . [they are] plans to prosper you and not to harm you, plans to give you hope and a future."*** The way to experience **"The Awesome Power of Joy"** is found in what you believe about yourself and your purpose for living. If you believe that you are God's child and that God has plans and a purpose for you, then you are open and ready to experience **"The Awesome Power of Joy."**

The "Awesome Power of Joy" in our lives is affected by what we believe about others.

I included this section because many people in our community withdraw and become isolated during holidays, either because of tragedies that may have happened around the holidays or because of personal angst and family issues. During the holidays, especially Christmas, we have no joy because we do not understand the importance of believing in others and building strong relationships with other people to sustain us and our emotional well-being. It is vitally important that each of us build strong, nurturing relationships with other people.

In a recent study, researchers at UC-Berkeley found that, during the holidays, socially isolated people were susceptible to illness, depression, and death at rates two to three times higher than people with richer social lives. Psychiatrist Dr. Robert Taylor makes this statement: **"When people have close relationships, they feel less threatened, less alone, more confident and more in control. Knowing you have people you can turn to in times of need can provide some very important feelings of security, optimism, and hope—all of which can be great antidotes to stress."[28]**

In other words, to help us experience **"The Awesome Power of Joy,"** it is very important that we develop close friendships and close relationships with other people. It is very important that we allow other people to be a part of our lives and that we become a part of the lives of others. I have found that, no matter how difficult I perceive my problem to be, just being able to talk about the problem with someone that I knew and trusted has always been enough to make my problem a little bit lighter. We have to believe that there are others out there pulling for us, wishing us only the best out of life, and willing to sacrifice a part of themselves so that we may live better lives. Some of us know these people as the family into which we were born. Some of us know these people as the "family" we have created around us after our birth families deserted us. But, no matter the origins of our family, we must learn to rely upon them as people who can and will help us during those times in our lives when we need help.

---

[28] "Love and our emotions on health." Alternative Health Resources – Your Information Site for the Natural Health Disciplines. <http://www.zhealthinfo.com/index.htm>

"The Awesome Power of Joy" is affected by what we believe about Jesus Christ.

Jesus **is** indeed the reason for the season. If you want to experience **"The Awesome Power of Joy,"** it starts with Jesus. In the gospel today, it says that John the Baptist came as a witness to the Light (Jesus Christ) so that all might believe. *Believe what?* Believe that Jesus Christ is the Son of God. Believe in and accept Jesus Christ as our Savior and Sovereign. But we also need to believe that Jesus Christ came that we **might have life and have it more abundantly**.[29] Included in life's abundance is **"The Awesome Power of Joy."** Jesus Christ did not come so that we would be downcast and downhearted; he came that we might be uplifted, filled with the joy that He places deep in our hearts.

On most Sundays our hymn of declaration is a slow, meditative, and worshipful praise chorus, but NOT today. On this third Sunday of Advent when the theme is Joy, I want us to raise our voices and sing with great vigor *"How Great Our Joy!"* Why? Because we do so as a testimony of the fact that what we believe about ourselves, what we believe about our purpose in living, what we believe about others, and what we believe about Jesus Christ will all help us to experience **"The Awesome Power of Joy."**

---

[29]Paraphrase of John 10:10 (KJV)("I am come that they might have life, and that they might have *it* more abundantly).

CHAPTER 10:
FRIENDSHIP AND THE
MEASURE OF LOVE

A sermon using the following scriptures:

THE EPISTLE TEXT: I John 3:11-20

[11] *This is the message you heard from the beginning: We should love one another.* [12] *Do not be like Cain, who belonged to the evil one and murdered his brother. And why did he murder him? Because his own actions were evil and his brother's were righteous.* [13] *Do not be surprised, my brothers, if the world hates you.* [14] *We know that we have passed from death to life, because we love our brothers. Anyone who does not love remains in death.* [15] *Anyone who hates his brother is a murderer, and you know that no murderer has eternal life in him.* [16] *This is how we know what love is: Jesus Christ laid down his life for us. And we ought to lay down our lives for our brothers.* [17] *If anyone has material possessions and sees his brother in need but has no pity on him, how can the love of God be in him?* [18] *Dear children, let us not love with words or tongue but with actions and in truth.* [19] *This then is how we know that we belong to the truth, and how we set our hearts at rest in his presence* [20] *whenever our hearts condemn us. For God is greater than our hearts, and he knows everything.*

THE GOSPEL TEXT: John 10: 7-11; 14-16

[7] *Therefore Jesus said again, "I tell you the truth, I am the gate for the sheep.* [8] *All who ever came before me were thieves and robbers, but the sheep did not listen to them.* [9] *I am the gate; whoever enters through me will be saved. He will come in and go out, and find pasture.* [10] *The thief*

comes only to steal and kill and destroy; I have come that they may have life, and have it to the full. ¹¹ *"I am the good shepherd. The good shepherd lays down his life for the sheep."*

¹⁴ *"I am the good shepherd; I know my sheep and my sheep know me--¹⁵just as the Father knows me and I know the Father--and I lay down my life for the sheep.* ¹⁶*I have other sheep that are not of this sheep pen. I must bring them also. They too will listen to my voice, and there shall be one flock and one shepherd.*

THE SERMON

Today is the fourth Sunday of Easter; it is also *Bring-A-Friend Sunday*[30] here at Covenant. We did not know it when we planned *Bring-A-Friend Sunday*, but the lectionary readings for today talk about the true measure of love and friendship. In John's Gospel, that true measure is described in terms of a good shepherd who is a friend of the sheep, one who will give his life for his sheep. The Epistle exhorts us to the highest levels of friendship that patterns itself after Jesus' love and friendship for us. It says, ***"we should love one another . . . This is how we know what love is: Jesus Christ laid down His life for us. And we ought to lay down our lives for our [friends]."***

It is said that friendship is manifested when the friend acts in some special way for you. Love is also manifested when a friend acts in some special way for you. If you are here

---

[30] *Bring-A-Friend Sunday* is a Covenant Community Church evangelistic outreach program similar to the better known "Each One Bring One: The Mission Andrew Principle."

today because you were invited or brought by a friend-- Welcome! Your friends manifested friendship and love to you because they wanted you to hear of God's unconditional love. They acted in a special way on your behalf. This morning I want to share with you a few things about **"Friendship and the Measure of Love."**

The models for "Friendship and the Measure of Love" come from God.

I was over at Southside Baptist Church last Monday for a meeting. While I was there I picked up a copy of the magazine, *Christian Ethics Today.* In it was a wonderful article, written by television commentator Bill Moyers, called *"Jesus has been hijacked."* (Unbeknownst to me, Bill Moyers is an ordained Baptist minister). In his article, Bill Moyers stated:

> **Make no mistake about it. The language of religion has been placed at the service of a partisan agenda. God is being invoked to undermine safeguards for public health and the environment, to demonize political opponents, to censor textbooks, to ostracize "the other," to end public funding for the arts, to cut taxes on the rich, and to misinform and mislead voters.[31]**

---

[31] Moyers, Bill. "Jesus Has Been Hijacked." *Christian Ethics Today – Journal of Christian Ethics*, Vol. 11, Issue 056, No. 4, Fall 2005. <http://www.christianethicstoday.com>

The article then makes this stark statement: **"The fact is, Jesus has been hijacked."** Well, our experiences in the LGBTQ community with many members of "Christian Right" organizations certainly confirm the truthfulness of the statements made by Bill Moyers. I just did not know that other people outside of our LGBTQ community were paying any attention to the phenomenon.

After I finished reading the article, I realized that God must have known that it would be a real struggle for us humans, yes, even for us Christians, to be the model of friendship and the measure of love that are really needed in our communities and in our world. So Jesus does not simply give us a model for friendship and the measure of love-- Jesus became and is Himself that model. God's love in Christ is the model! God wants to be awakened in us, so that we might have the ability to love ourselves and others with the full measure set as examples by Jesus. And, how do we do that?

"Friendship and the Measure of Love" require us to remain connected to the source of love.

That statement makes as good a case as any as to why we need friends and why we need to regularly attend a church that affirms the measure of God's love in us. God is the source of love. The Apostle John says it clearly, ***"God is love."***[32] There are not many places in this world where we are constantly reminded that we are special to God, that we are unique and wonderful in God's sight, and that we are crowned with glory and honor as children of God. I talk about the unconditional love of God so much around our

---

[32] 1 John 4:8.

church because so many people, especially in our community, need to hear it again and again, to counteract all those messages out there coming at us every day saying just the opposite. Jesus said, *"the thief comes only to steal and kill and destroy; I have come that they may have life, and have it to the full[est]."*

We need to come to the realization that not everyone wants us to "have life to the fullest," a statement that is true whether you are a member of the LGBTQ community or not. But, especially in the LGBTQ community, we see attempts made to place additional civil and legal obstacles in our paths each and every day. It is an effort to deny our community the ability to have life to the fullest that fuels the laws and constitutional amendments against gay marriage, that writes the laws denying otherwise qualified persons the right to adopt children (based simply upon their sexual orientation) and that, in so many jobs, denies any legal protection to persons who have been fired because of their sexual orientation or transgendered status, so long as the employer can come up with a pretext for the firing.

How do we have life to the fullest in the face of such things? How do we survive this constant damage to our psyche, avoid developing low self-esteem, and avoid hating the folks who are doing these things to us? We do it by reaching out to each other and building relationships of friendship among ourselves. We do it by strengthening the bonds of love among ourselves. We do it by remaining connected to the One who loves us unconditionally. When we do this, we can respond to our adversaries with God's measure of love and friendship.

God's desire is for us to live out the reality of love. It is a love that returns to us. We can live as Jesus said, *"life to the fullest"* when we build relationships and friendships with others and when we refuse to allow other people to dictate who we are or cause us to hate. **This type of life is possible, if we get connected and remain connected to the source of love--God.**

"Friendship and the Measure of Love" require commitment and sacrifice.

I know that commitment and sacrifice are not popular terms these days. But I cannot talk about friendship and the measure of love without addressing commitment and sacrifice. The scripture in I John says, *"This is how we know what love is; Jesus Christ laid down His life for us. And we ought to lay down our lives for our [friends]. Dear [friends], let us not love with words or tongue but with actions and in truth."[33]*

John is talking about a friendship and about the measure of love which include commitment and sacrifice, because that was exactly what Jesus did for us. In John 15, Jesus calls His disciples "friends" immediately after describing the greatest love as one person willing to lay down his or her life for a friend. Jesus says that is the measure of love and friendship that God honors and to which we are called.

The truth is that not many of us will be called upon to lay down our lives for a friend. But, from time to time, we are called upon to display a commitment of love and sacrifice by going the extra mile for a friend. We are called upon to

---

[33] 1 John 3:16 & 18 (NIV®). (Inclusiveness added).

share with our neighbors in times of need, even though we may be in need ourselves. We are called upon to be a source of strength and comfort for our friends and neighbors, even when all we want to do is go somewhere and be comforted ourselves. On rare occasions, we are called upon to stand with and support our friends, family, or neighbors in unpopular situations, because doing so is the "right" thing to do. These small sacrifices are some of the ways that we can love with "actions and truth."

This Sunday is Bring-A-Friend Sunday at Covenant and we are glad that all of you are here. We are grateful that your friends invited you here. It is our heart's desire that each of you will come to know the full measure of God's love. It is our heart's desire that each of you will come to really know God as a friend, someone to whom you can relate and someone you can trust. If you do, it will be a friendship like none you have ever experienced before and it will be with unconditional love and love without measure.

You see, our model for **"Friendship and the Measure of Love"** comes directly from God through the life and death of God's son, Jesus Christ. We, too, can be a source of love for our friends and neighbors, just as Christ is a source of love for us. As we strengthen the bonds of love between ourselves and our friends, we also strengthen the connections with God's love. We need to remain connected to God's love as a source, even though true friendship and love require commitment and sacrifice. But, is not that what Christ offers us? Christ made the sacrifice of laying down his life for his friends. Very few of us will ever be called to lay down our lives, but, at some point, all of us will be called to be a source of strength, a source of comfort, or a source of love for our friends. When we remain connected to the source of our strength—God--we are able to demonstrate through our lives the true **"Friendship and the Measure of Love."**

CHAPTER 11:
EASTER – WHAT A DIFFERENCE
A DAY MAKES!

A sermon using the following Scriptures:

THE EPISTLE TEXT: Romans 6:8-11 & 14

[8] Now if we died with Christ, we believe that we will also live with him. [9] For we know that since Christ was raised from the dead, he cannot die again; death no longer has mastery over him. [10] The death he died, he died to sin once for all; but the life he lives, he lives to God. [11] In the same way, count yourselves dead to sin but alive to God in Christ Jesus.

[14] For sin shall not be your master, because you are not under law, but under grace.

THE GOSPEL TEXT: Matthew 28:1-10

[1] After the Sabbath, at dawn on the first day of the week, Mary Magdalene and the other Mary went to look at the tomb. [2] There was a violent earthquake, for an angel of the Lord came down from heaven and, going to the tomb, rolled back the stone and sat on it. [3] His appearance was like lightning, and his clothes were white as snow. [4] The guards were so afraid of him that they shook and became like dead men. [5] The angel said to the women, "Do not be afraid, for I know that you are looking for Jesus, who was crucified. [6] He is not here; he has risen, just as he said. Come and see the place where he lay. [7] Then go quickly and tell his disciples: 'He has risen from the dead and is going ahead of you into Galilee. There you will see him.' Now I have told you." [8] So the women hurried away from the tomb, afraid yet filled with joy, and ran to tell his

disciples. ⁹Suddenly Jesus met them. "Greetings," he said. They came to him, clasped his feet and worshipped him. ¹⁰Then Jesus said to them, "Do not be afraid. Go and tell my brothers to go to Galilee; there they will see me."

THE SERMON

Happy Easter! Christ the Lord has risen today indeed, Alleluia! **"What A Difference A Day Makes!"**

This past Friday, Good Friday morning, I joined a group of ministers and other advocates who work on behalf of the poor and homeless here in our city. We did a two and one-half hour Good Friday Stations of the Cross procession through downtown Birmingham. The stations in which we stopped were places that helped the poor, places where the poor gather, and places where the poor experience oppression. Several of us were assigned to designated stations and given pre-assigned scriptures and our task was to preach a short sermon about how we continue to crucify Christ today through our indifference to, abuse of, and injustice to the poor. My assignment was to preach at the **Firehouse Shelter**, and I was honored to be included. It was a very moving and a very solemn experience.

On Good Friday evening we observed the 14 Stations of the Cross here at Covenant. At the end, we quietly left the sanctuary to enter into our Easter Vigil commemorating and remembering the time Jesus spent in the grave. The mood for that occasion also was very solemn.

Finally on that same day, we held our Good Friday Tenebrae Service. It too was a very moving service, but with a mood of solemnity. As we quietly left the sanctuary in the dark, some left with heavy hearts, while others left in tears, thinking of what Christ had endured for us and our salvation.

Our solemn mood continued on Saturday. The choir presented its annual Easter Cantata and the Joyful Souls acting troupe performed its Easter drama, both again reminding us of the suffering that Jesus endured on our behalf.

But **"What A Difference A Day Makes!"** Today is Easter Sunday! Our mood is no longer solemn because we have read the end of the story. We know that Jesus lives and we win. Our mood has gone from the solemnity of Good Friday and the Saturday Easter Vigil to pure, absolute joy because today is *a celebration of the resurrection.* So today, let us reflect upon **"What A Difference A Day Makes!"**

On Friday, Jesus, the Son of God, died on a cross. His followers were devastated and they scattered. In despair, they went into hiding. Saturday, Jesus spent the entire day in the tomb. If you have ever had someone close to you to die, then you know how that second day can be worse than the first day! Often the true magnitude of the loss does not begin to sink in until that second day, and the weight of grief is compounded. As bad as Jesus' death on the Cross was for His followers on Friday, in all likelihood, the Saturday was probably even worse, as they tried to come to some understanding and acceptance of what had happened to Jesus.

But, **"What A Difference A Day Makes!"** Sunday morning, the two Marys came to the tomb to visit the final resting place of a dead friend; instead, they discovered a risen Lord!! The angel said to them, *"I know that you are looking for Jesus, who was crucified. He is NOT here; He has risen, as He said. Come see the place where He laid."* Then the angel sent the women disciples to tell the men disciples the good news and on their way to do so, the women disciples suddenly met Jesus. They *"came to Him, clasped His feet and worshipped Him."* Hallelujah! **"What A Difference A Day Makes!"**

This Easter, some of us need to remember that this day is a celebration of the Resurrection. And, some of us are in dire need of a resurrection in many areas of our lives. Some of us gathered here today are afflicted in mind or body by some kind of sickness, virus, disease, or medical hardship. We need to know today that the God, who resurrected Jesus Christ, can also resurrect complete and total health in our minds and bodies.

Some of us gathered here today may be struggling to keep a special relationship together, or struggling for acceptance in our families, or struggling with an addiction, or perhaps struggling with unemployment or under-employment. We need to know this day is a celebration of the resurrection and that the God who resurrected Jesus Christ can resurrect wholeness in your lives.

Some of us gathered here today may be struggling against failure in our lives, disappointment, roadblocks, detours, and dead-end streets. No matter where we turn, it seems to be the wrong way or a poor choice. **But, "What A**

Difference A Day Makes!" We need to know that this is a celebration of the Resurrection and that Jesus Christ, resurrected from the dead, can resurrect in us hope for a better and more abundant life.

There is nothing too hard for God, and scripture tells us that all we have to do is ask in the name of Jesus and believe that we will receive. The God who resurrected Jesus Christ can resurrect, in our lives, all that we need to live happy and fulfilling lives.

I think about the story of the elderly woman who was well known both for her faith and her boldness in proclaiming her faith. She would stand on her front porch and shout **"Praise the Lord! Praise the Lord!"** Next door to her lived an atheist who would get so angry at her for her outcries. So he would shout back, **"There ain't no Lord!"** **"There ain't no Lord!"** Once, when hard times had fallen upon this elderly woman, she prayed for God to send her some needed assistance. She stood on her porch and shouted, **"Praise the Lord. God, I need food! I am having a hard time. Please, Lord, send me some groceries!!"**

The next morning the elderly woman found several bags on her front porch. She looked in the bags and saw groceries and began to shout at the top of her lungs, **"Praise the Lord for all His good bounty toward me!"** The atheist neighbor jumped from behind a bush and said, **"Aha! I told you there was no Lord. I brought those groceries, God didn't!"** Immediately, the elderly woman starting jumping up and down, clapping her hands and shouting,

"Praise the Lord! God not only sent me groceries, but He made the devil pay for them! Praise the Lord!"

"What A Difference A Day Makes!" One day, the elderly woman was hungry and in need. However, the next day she had an abundance of food and she had no doubt about the source of her help!! That elderly woman knew that God is able to provide everything we need, even though what we need might come from some unlikely sources!

Jesus died on the cross of Calvary for our salvation, our wholeness, and our well-being. That means that Jesus is interested in our spiritual as well as our physical needs. That is why I love that song "*When He Was On The Cross – I Was on His Mind*,"[34] because the chorus joyfully reminds us that we have always been special to Jesus, our Lord and Saviour. Jesus went to hell on our behalf and the scriptures tell us that it was so that He might triumph over death, hell, and the grave on our behalf. **"What A Difference A Day Makes!"** After being in hell all that Saturday, Jesus arose from the dead on Easter Sunday. He lives so that we might have abundance and like the old woman said, *"He even made the devil pay for it."*

Let me leave you with three short points this Easter Sunday of "What A Difference A Day Makes!" and why today is a celebration of the resurrection:

---

[34] Payne, Ronald Michael and Ronnie Hinson (Words and Music). "When He Was on the Cross – I Was on His Mind." Wind in Willow Publishing (BMI)(Administered by ICG)/Songs of Calvary (BMI), 1984.

Easter declares that God always has the last word, not Satan.

You may think there is no hope for your situation, whatever it is, but today is a celebration of the resurrection, and because He Lives, there is hope for you. God always has the last word, even over death. You can become a beneficiary of God's awesome power, if you will open your life to God and your heart to the hope magnified through the resurrection of Jesus Christ.

Because He lives, instead of living our lives as prisoners of guilt, we now can live as the forgiven people of God.

Guilt controls a larger portion of our lives than we would ever want to admit. Some of us today need to understand that nothing we have ever done is beyond the forgiveness of God. God knows us at our worst and still loves us. The Epistle lesson from Romans emphasized this blessed truth by saying, *"The death that Jesus died, Jesus died to sin once for all; but the life Christ lives, He lives to God. In the same way, (because Jesus died for us) count yourselves dead to sin but alive to God in Christ Jesus. For sin shall not be your master, because you are not under the law, but under grace."* Jesus died and rose again so that we might live free of guilt as the forgiven people of God.

Because He lives, Easter Sunday assures us that we can live as victors rather than victims!

Jesus died on the cross, but the story does not end there. Christ rose on the third day, a victor over the grave! In

Jesus Christ, we are victors over all adversity that confronts us.

If you have never given your problems, pains, and worries (whatever they are) over to God, then you might feel like a victim of this world. But, you should not have to accept this victim status. How tragic it is for believers to continue to fight the "Good Friday" battle and always remain victims rather than to claim the power of "Resurrection Sunday" and become victors through Jesus Christ!!

However, for those of us who understand the good news of Christ's resurrection, we sing:

I serve a risen Savior, He's in the world today,
I know that He is living, whatever men may say.
I see His hand of mercy, I hear His voice of cheer,
And just the time I need Him, He's always near.

He lives, He lives, Christ Jesus lives today!
He walks with me and talks with me, along life's
narrow way.
He lives, He lives, salvation to impart!
You ask me how I know He lives,
He lives within my heart.[35]

For most of us, there will be times in our lives when the night finds us in despair. It seems that we cannot make it through the night, and, certainly, we do not want to face the morning. But, we must always remember that we serve a

---

[35]Ackley, Alfred H. (Words and Music) and Sid Richardson (Arrangement). "He Lives." Belwin-Mills Publishing Corp., 1999.

risen Saviour who is interested in our total wholeness and well-being. Put your faith in God, through the resurrected son, Jesus Christ, who lives! If you have faith, and persevere through the night, you will be astonished at the joy that comes in the morning. You will come to understand the full measure of **"What A Difference A Day Makes!"**

PART IV:
A VISION FOR LIVING

"To be an inclusive community of faith –
'Offering Hope + Showing Faithfulness + Sharing Joy.'"
(Covenant Community Church's Vision Statement)

At Covenant, we believe that the highest form of worship is found in our service to others. To underscore that belief, at Covenant we often remind each other of that fact by using the humorous little line *"it ain't all about you."* That statement is further reinforced each summer in a three-part sermon series on the vision statement of our church.

I believe it is absolutely essential to keep the collective vision of the local church before the people. Therefore, Part IV - *"A Vision for Living,"* includes sermons that make the point that not only our church but every Christian is called to a life of serving others by *"Offering Hope + Showing Faithfulness + Sharing Joy."* This Covenant vision sermon series encourages us in a philosophy that has become "a core value" for our congregation and that is reflected in Galatians 6:9-10: *"Let us not become weary in doing good, for at the proper time we will reap a harvest if we do not give up. Therefore, as we have opportunity, <u>let us do good to all people</u>, especially to those who belong to the family of believers."* (Emphasis added).

CHAPTER 12:
THE VISION OF OFFERING HOPE

A Sermon using the following scriptures:

THE EPISTLE TEXT: Galatians 1:1-2, 7-12

[1]*Paul, an apostle--sent not from men nor by man, but by Jesus Christ and God the Father, who raised him from the dead--* [2]*and all the brothers with me. . . .*

[7]*Evidently some people are throwing you into confusion and are trying to pervert the gospel of Christ.* [8]*But even if we or an angel from heaven should preach a gospel other than the one we preached to you, let him be eternally condemned!* [9]*As we have already said, so now I say again: If anybody is preaching to you a gospel other than what you accepted, let him be eternally condemned!* [10]*Am I now trying to win the approval of men, or of God? Or am I trying to please men? If I were still trying to please men, I would not be a servant of Christ.* [11]*I want you to know, brothers, that the gospel I preached is not something that man made up.* [12]*I did not receive it from any man, nor was I taught it; rather, I received it by revelation from Jesus Christ.*

THE GOSPEL TEXT: Luke 10:1-12

[1]*After this the Lord appointed seventy-two others and sent them two by two ahead of him to every town and place where he was about to go.* [2]*He told them, "The harvest is plentiful, but the workers are few. Ask the Lord of the harvest, therefore, to send out workers into his harvest field.* [3]*Go! I am sending you out like lambs among wolves.* [4]*Do not take a purse or bag or sandals; and do not greet anyone on the road.* [5]*"When you enter a house, first say,*

'Peace to this house.' ⁶If a man of peace is there, your peace will rest on him; if not, it will return to you. ⁷Stay in that house, eating and drinking whatever they give you, for the worker deserves his wages. Do not move around from house to house. ⁸"When you enter a town and are welcomed, eat what is set before you. ⁹Heal the sick who are there and tell them, 'The kingdom of God is near you.' ¹⁰But when you enter a town and are not welcomed, go into its streets and say, ¹¹'Even the dust of your town that sticks to our feet we wipe off against you. Yet be sure of this: The kingdom of God is near.' ¹²I tell you, it will be more bearable on that day for Sodom than for that town.

THE SERMON

Today is the sixth Sunday after Pentecost, and we are beyond the halfway mark of both the liturgical and calendar years. So now it seems to be a good time for us to review our Covenant vision. Starting today, I am preaching a three part sermon series on our Church vision. Our vision statement is as follows: ***"To be an inclusive community of faith,* 'Offering Hope + Showing Faithfulness + Sharing Joy.'"*** Today let us talk about the first part of our vision statement in a message called **"The Vision of Offering Hope."**

The scriptures say *"Without a vision, the people perish."*[36] However, several religious leaders have rephrased this scripture to say, *"Without a vision, the people find another*

---

[36] Proverbs 29:18 (*The Holy Bible, King James Version*)(slightly paraphrased).

parish." Both statements are true and both statements show why we need to, at times, revisit our Covenant vision.

American author and poet, Arthur Tugman, penned a little poem that puts vision in this perspective:

> **There's something about vision**
> **When coupled with belief and written down in ink**
> **That lets you see further**
> **Than anyone else can think.**[37]

Therefore, knowing just how important a vision is, let us think about what it means for Covenant when we speak of **"The Vision of Offering Hope."** Both the Epistle and the Gospel lessons for today provide us with valuable information about offering hope.

In the Epistle from Galatians, Paul focuses on offering hope in the context of the responsibilities we have towards others within our own Christian Fellowship. In the Gospel lesson from Luke, offering hope is found in the context of reaching outside the household of faith to the larger community, like Jesus did in sending out the 70 disciples.

So, what does **"The Vision of Offering Hope"** mean for us today, within our church family and within our community at large? I want us to consider three things:

---

[37] Tugman, Arthur. "Vision." *AuthorsDen*.com. 24 June 2006. – <http://www.authorsden.com/visit/viewPoetry.asp?id=162483>

A "Vision of Offering Hope" begins by _putting our trust in Jesus._

Luke 10:3-4 says: *"Go! I am sending you out like lambs among wolves. Do not take a purse or bag or sandals; and do not greet anyone on the road."* (*I know that some of our more creative people have issues with that statement. After all, if Jesus sent certain members of this congregation on a missionary trip and told them not to take a purse, bag, or sandals, I know that would automatically disqualify half of "the queens" from becoming missionaries.*) But Jesus also says, *"Do not greet anyone on the road."* Many theologians believe that when Jesus said, *"do not greet anyone on the road"* he does NOT mean "do not speak to others as you meet them," but, rather, "do not gather from the people you meet along the way things you think you are going to need." That second interpretation certainly makes more sense as you read the text.

The point of this text is this: do not take all of these things with you and do not gather them along the way; rather, trust God for all your needs. Jesus sent these 70 disciples out defenseless, totally dependent on Him and on the reception of the people to whom Jesus sent them. They were to carry no cash, no spare clothes, and no provisions. **Offering hope for them required total trust in Jesus.**

What role does Jesus' example play in our Covenant **"Vision of Offering Hope?"** Well, our **"Vision of Offering Hope"** to our community also calls for us to have a radical trust in Jesus. Many of our folks walk in spiritual isolation because of the teachings of many other Christian churches. So a **"Vision of Offering Hope"** for us means trusting Jesus enough so as to NOT take our spiritual baggage with us when we go into our community trying to reach others with the good news of Jesus Christ. We are called upon to carry the word of God's unconditional love to a community that has not been told about His love. A lot of what we are doing is trying to counteract what our folks have learned in church. So a **"Vision of Offering Hope"** for us means trusting Jesus and not relying on church traditions, denominational security, or even the religious trappings of church as many of us have known it in our past. We are to cease trusting in our own resources and begin to trust completely in God's love for us. **A "Vision of Offering Hope" means learning to _radically put our trust in Jesus_.**

A "Vision of Offering Hope" means standing firm in the face of opposition.

Look at Jesus' instructions to His disciples in verses 10 and 11. *"But when you enter a town and are not welcomed, go into the streets and say, 'Even the dust of your town that sticks to our feet we wipe off against you. Yet be sure of this: The kingdom of God is near.'"* Jesus told his disciples that they would encounter opposition. Therefore, we also know to expect opposition, especially when our vision is one of *"being an inclusive community of faith 'Offering Hope.'"* But, remember, God has called us to this vision and that means standing firm even in the face of opposition, no matter the source of that opposition!

We are all very familiar with the opposition to our **"Vision of Offering Hope"** that comes from other churches, governments, and even society at large. I got a lengthy e-mail this week from someone just "coming out." I just want to share a little of the e-mail with you because the end of the e-mail mentions the opposition our community routinely experiences. He begins by saying **"Dear Pastor J.R., I just wanted to thank you, and all of Covenant, for the welcome I received when visiting this past Sunday morning and evening. It was my second visit, and I always find myself fed, refreshed, and encouraged."** After sharing a bit of his story, he concludes his email with these words: **"Your work . . . is so important. The witness of Covenant as a place of love and acceptance in a city and state that bears little enough goodwill toward gays and lesbians is likewise invaluable. As a man only recently out, and not really a bar scene kind of guy, a place like Covenant, where I can experience community, is precious. God bless you and thank you!"** This man and thousands like him in this city are the reasons we *put our trust in Jesus and stand firm even in the face of opposition* to our "Vision of Offering Hope."

Our "Vision of Offering Hope" offers Christ as the hope for a better life.

The gospel text from Luke 10:8-9 says: *"when you enter a town and are welcomed, eat what is set before you. Heal the sick who are there and tell them, 'the kingdom of God is near you.'"* In other words, do not get hung up with side issues; keep focused on the main thing--**the main thing**--and do not belabor the small stuff. Remember your **"Vision of Offering Hope"** and remember that your mission is offering Jesus Christ as the hope for a better life.

Later in the book of Galatians, the Apostle Paul takes the concept of offering hope a bit further and gives some practical advice as to how we stay true to our **"Vision of Offering Hope"** and how we offer Christ as the hope for a better life. The scripture says: *"[I]f someone is caught in a sin . . . restore him [or her] gently . . . . Carry each other's burdens, and in this way you will fulfill the law of Christ."*[38] Too often we meet people whose lives have spiraled out of control. They do not know where to turn, where to go, or what to do. Yet, for too many of them, when they have tried to turn to God, all they received in many churches was guilt-based religion.

The daughter of one of our members recently graduated from high school. It was a very proud moment in the daughter's life, but even more so in our member's life. Our member's mother (based upon her own guilt-based religious beliefs) had predicted that, simply because our member got divorced, our member's daughter would never complete high school!! As we share in our member's happiness, we recognize and appreciate the importance of offering hope. Hope is not offered through negative predictions and prognostications, but through positive encouragement and love.

I could rattle off countless examples of similar experiences that members of our community face on a daily basis. But, I think you see why it is important for our community to have Covenant offering Christ as the hope for a better life. Because of our **"Vision of Offering Hope,"** we do not believe in guilt-based salvation. If someone has made a mistake, even a serious one, we do not beat them up. We

---

[38] Galatians 6:1-2.

will try to correct them by showing them a better way. Yes, we believe that everyone is accountable for his or her actions, and we know that there are consequences for everything we do in life. However, we try to correct people by holding them accountable in ways that lifts them up, so that they may see their better selves. We know that very few people are helped when you beat them down. Our **"Vision of Offering Hope"** helps because it **offers Christ as the hope for a better life.**

Here at Covenant, we have a **"Vision of Offering Hope."** It is what we do and it is what the Epistle lesson from Galatians encourages, exhorts, and cajoles us to do continually. In Galatians 5:9-10, the Epistle lesson says: *"Let us not become weary in doing good* (offering hope), *for at the proper time we will reap a harvest if we do not give up. Therefore, as we have opportunity, let us do good* (offer hope) *to all people, especially to the family of believers* (our community). *"*

If you hope for a better life for yourself, your birth family, your church family, and our community, I tell you **without reservation** that Christ is the answer. The answer begins with understanding first and foremost that God loves each of us. Because of God's love, at Covenant, we are *"an inclusive community of faith"* with **"A Vision of Offering Hope."** We do that by:

1) **Putting our trust in Jesus,**
2) **Standing firm in the face of opposition, and**
3) **Offering Christ as the Hope for a better life.**

CHAPTER 13:
THE VISION OF SHOWING FAITHFULNESS

A sermon using the following scriptures:

THE EPISTLE TEXT: Colossians 1:2, 10-12

²To the holy and faithful brothers in Christ at Colosse: Grace and Peace to you from God our father.

¹⁰And we pray this in order that you may live a life worthy of the Lord and may please him in every way: bearing fruit in every good work, growing in the knowledge of God, ¹¹being strengthened with all power according to his glorious might so that you may have great endurance and patience, and joyfully ¹²giving thanks to the Father, who has qualified you to share in the inheritance of the saints in the kingdom of light.

THE GOSPEL TEXT: Luke 10:25-37

²⁵On one occasion an expert in the law stood up to test Jesus. "Teacher," he asked, "what must I do to inherit eternal life?" ²⁶"What is written in the Law?" he replied. "How do you read it?" ²⁷He answered: "'Love the Lord your God with all your heart and with all your soul and with all your strength and with all your mind'; and, 'Love your neighbor as yourself.'" ²⁸"You have answered correctly," Jesus replied. "Do this and you will live." ²⁹But he wanted to justify himself, so he asked Jesus, "And who is my neighbor?" ³⁰In reply Jesus said: "A man was going down from Jerusalem to Jericho, when he fell into the hands of robbers. They stripped him of his clothes, beat him and went away, leaving him half dead. ³¹A priest happened to be going down the same road, and when he saw the man, he passed by on the other side. ^{32}*So too, a Levite, when he came to the place and saw him, passed by on the other side.* ^{33}*But a Samaritan, as he traveled, came where the man was; and when he saw him, he took pity on him.* ^{34}*He went to him and bandaged his wounds, pouring on oil and wine. Then he put the man on his own donkey, took him to an inn and took care of him.* ^{35}*The next day he took out two silver coins and gave them to the innkeeper. 'Look after him,' he said, 'and when I return, I will reimburse you for any extra expense you may have.'* ^{36}*"Which of these three do you think was a neighbor to the man who fell into the hands of robbers?"* ^{37}*The expert in the law replied, "The one who had mercy on him." Jesus told him, "Go and do likewise."*

THE SERMON

On this Seventh Sunday after Pentecost, we are at the midway point in my three-week sermon series on our Covenant vision statement. Our Covenant vision is *"To be an inclusive community of faith* 'Offering Hope + Showing Faithfulness + Sharing Joy.'"

In the first sermon, **"The Vision of Offering Hope,"** we learned that we fulfilled the vision of offering hope by:

1) **Putting our Trust in Jesus;**
2) **Standing Firm in the face of opposition; and,**
3) **Offering Christ as the Hope for a New Life.**

In this sermon, we look at the second part of our vision statement – "*Showing Faithfulness.*" In today's message, **"The Vision of Showing Faithfulness,"** I want to concentrate on the practical, day-to-day ways to show our faithfulness to God and each other through how we live and what we do.

The Colossian text today tells us how to live when we have a "**Vision of Showing Faithfulness**," and provides us with the motivation for doing so. Paul says, "*we pray this in order that you may live a life worthy of the Lord and may please [the Lord] in every way: <u>bearing fruit in every good work</u>. . .*" Showing faithfulness is about living a life worthy of and pleasing to the Lord. That life is one that bears fruit by your good works.

The story of the Good Samaritan, found in the gospel today, is an excellent example of faithfulness. Most of us know the story well. Jesus tells about a man traveling from Jerusalem to Jericho. On the way he fell among robbers, who stripped him, beat him, and left him half dead. The distance on this road from Jerusalem to Jericho was approximately 17 miles and muggings on this road often occurred. So here lay this unfortunate man, in desperate straits, beaten, probably bloody, naked, and the scriptures say, "half dead." The scriptures then tell us that first a priest and then a Levite came upon the man and saw his condition. However, both of these religious leaders passed the man by and continued on their way. In fact, the scriptures point out that both these religious leaders passed by "on the other side." It does not matter that it was Jewish religious leaders who passed by the desperate man. Jesus could have easily said a Baptist pastor or a Catholic priest passed by the man. Insensitivity to the plight of others is not limited to any particular race, creed, or religion.

Regardless of their religious affiliation, they should have known and should have done better.

The hero of this story was a Samaritan, which was even more shocking to Jesus' listeners. The relations between Jews and Samaritans were so strained that it made it even more surprising that a Samaritan would offer a Jew this kind of assistance. This very familiar story offers us excellent guidance on what it means when we have **"The Vision of Showing Faithfulness."**

Showing faithfulness means bearing fruit in every good work even when no reward is anticipated.

Too often people only do things when they are getting some reward or benefit for doing so. But showing faithfulness is bearing fruit **without** expecting or anticipating anything in return. The Good Samaritan did not know the wounded traveler; nor did the Good Samaritan have any expectation that he would receive any reward for his kindness to the wounded traveler. However, the sad plight of the wounded traveler clearly touched the Good Samaritan's heart and the Good Samaritan exhibited his love and compassion for his fellow man by **"showing faithfulness"** through his actions.

Most of the time when we think about this story, we concentrate primarily on the Good Samaritan himself. However, there is another strong example of faithfulness in the story. Let's look at the actions of the innkeeper. Try to imagine carrying a beaten and bloodied man to the Marriott Hotel downtown and saying to the manager, **"This poor man is going to need some looking after. Here is some**

money. Take care of this man while I am gone and if this does not cover all of the expenses, I will reimburse you when I return." *What do you think the manager's response would be?* This parable of Jesus could have also been called "*The Kind Innkeeper*" as well as "*The Good Samaritan.*" The innkeeper did not have to take on the additional responsibility of a badly beaten guest, particularly since the innkeeper did not know the circumstances surrounding the wounded traveler's injuries and could not be certain that the Good Samaritan would return as he promised. However, the Bible records no words of protest from the innkeeper. Instead, we are presented with a picture of the innkeeper **"showing faithfulness"** by willingly accepting the additional duties.

Even now, God has a way of giving us the perfect example of showing faithfulness. Recently, there was a television news broadcast regarding the expulsion of a two year old boy and his family from a campground in South Alabama because the two year old is infected with HIV. The little two year old boy is one of the foster children of a very loving couple. In addition to the HIV status of the two year old, the foster father has terminal cancer.

This expulsion of the family caught the attention of a member of our congregation. I got an e-mail from this person this week. Our member wants to help that family experience a wonderful vacation here in Birmingham, but wishes to remain totally anonymous. Therefore, our member wants the arrangements for the vacation to be made through the church. From a worldly standpoint, our member receives nothing in return, not even the recognition from the family that most of us would crave. But from a spiritual standpoint, I could not have dreamed up a better example for us. It says everything that needs to be said about **"A Vision of Showing Faithfulness is bearing fruit in every good work, even when no reward is anticipated."**

Showing faithfulness means being sensitive to the needs of the people we encounter.

The story of our anonymous benefactor, like the story of the Good Samaritan and the Kind Innkeeper, is a call to "well doing." These stories remind us that kindness and decency are possible in this world when we are sensitive to the needs of others we encounter.

After Jesus taught that we should love our neighbors as ourselves, Jesus was asked, *"Who is my neighbor?"* In response, Jesus told the story of the Good Samaritan and then answered the question with a question: *"Which one of these three do you think was a neighbor to the man who fell into the hands of the robbers?"* . . . *The expert in the law replied, 'The one who had mercy on him.'"* Jesus told him, **"Go and do likewise."**

It is interesting that it is the Samaritan--the outcast, the disenfranchised, the marginalized, and the ostracized person in this story--who practiced the great commandment to *"Love the Lord your God will all your heart and with all your soul and with all your strength and with all your mind; and Love your neighbor as yourself."* The use of this story was deliberate on the part of Jesus because Jesus does not care whether you are a member of the right church or belong to the right group; instead, Jesus is concerned with whether you are living **"The Vision of Showing Faithfulness."** When we love God with all our hearts and love our neighbors as ourselves, we become aware of the needs of others around us. **Showing faithfulness means being sensitive to the needs of the people we encounter. Showing faithfulness is about having the compassion and the courage to act and to do what needs to be done.**

In Colossians 1:10, the Apostle Paul says *"we pray this in order that you may live a life worthy of the Lord and may please [the Lord] in every way: <u>bearing fruit in every good work</u> . . . ."* After having told the story of the Good Samaritan and the Kind Innkeeper and having asked the question which one of the three--the priest, the Levite or the Samaritan--was a neighbor to the person in need, Jesus concluded the lesson in Luke by telling the expert in the law to *"[g]o and do likewise."*

When I heard the story about the two year old and how he and his family had been ostracized by a group of people who should have known better, I was outraged. I am sure some people who heard the story wanted to go stage a protest march against the people who did this horrible thing to a two-year old little boy and his family. No doubt our anonymous benefactor was also outraged, but, rather than just being outraged, our anonymous benefactor channeled that outrage into compassion and the courage to act by being a real neighbor.

Kay Hendricks, our Minister of Congregational Care, made contact with the foster mother of the two year old on behalf of our anonymous benefactor. Surprisingly, Kay did not find a person who was bitter and unforgiving about what had happened to her family. Understandably, the foster mother could not believe that someone in this day could be so ignorant about the ways HIV is contracted that they could think that her two year old foster son posed a risk of infecting others. But then she took the time to be a neighbor and was gracious enough to acknowledge that maybe the people who committed this act down there in rural South Alabama just lacked the education as to how HIV is transmitted. Additionally, the foster mother also said that she just could not believe that someone who did not know them or their son would be so kind as to offer them a wonderful, and very much needed, vacation. In a voice filled with gratitude and amazement, the foster mother said to Kay, **"There really are caring people in this world, aren't there?"** Kay responded **"Yes, there are!"**

Showing faithfulness means living a life worthy and pleasing to the Lord, bearing fruit in every good work. That wonderful anonymous person that I talked about this morning knows something about being a good neighbor and a Good Samaritan. It means living **"A Vision of Showing Faithfulness"** by:

1) **Bearing fruit in every good work, even when no reward is anticipated,**
2) **Being sensitive to the needs of the people we encounter, and**
3) **Having the compassion and the courage to act and to do what needs to be done.**

Jesus' question to us today is *"To whom do you need to be a neighbor?"* In our church membership class yesterday, I stressed what it means to be a member of this church.

Among other important things, membership means learning to be a good neighbor in our community. So think about it. *"To whom do you need to be a good neighbor?" Can you reach out to them without looking for something in return? Can you be sensitive to that person's needs? Do you have the compassion and the courage to do what needs to be done in that person's life?*

I pray this morning that your answer will go something like this one: "I will show faithfulness to you God, by being a neighbor to whoever needs me." Perhaps the words of this little chorus can be your answer, **"I will serve thee, because I love thee[.] You have given life to me."**[39] That type of service is what happens when we have **"The Vision of Showing Faithfulness."**

---

[39]Gaither, William J. (Words and Music) and Gloria Gaither (Words). "I Will Serve Thee." Gaither Copyright Management, 1969.

CHAPTER 14:
THE VISION OF SHARING JOY

A sermon using the following scriptures:

THE EPISTLE TEXT: I John 4:7-12, 16-21

[7]*Dear friends, let us love one another, for love comes from God. Everyone who loves has been born of God and knows God.* [8]*Whoever does not love does not know God, because God is love.* [9]*This is how God showed his love among us: He sent his one and only Son into the world that we might live through him.* [10]*This is love: not that we loved God, but that he loved us and sent his Son as an atoning sacrifice for our sins.* [11]*Dear friends, since God so loved us, we also ought to love one another.* [12]*No one has ever seen God; but if we love one another, God lives in us and his love is made complete in us.*

[16]*And so we know and rely on the love God has for us. God is love. Whoever lives in love lives in God, and God in him.* [17]*In this way, love is made complete among us so that we will have confidence on the day of judgment, because in this world we are like him.* [18]*There is no fear in love. But perfect love drives out fear, because fear has to do with punishment. The one who fears is not made perfect in love.* [19]*We love because he first loved us.* [20]*If anyone says, "I love God," yet hates his brother, he is a liar. For anyone who does not love his brother, whom he has seen, cannot love God, whom he has not seen.* [21]*And he has given us this command: Whoever loves God must also love his brother.*

THE GOSPEL TEXT: Luke 10:38-42

[38]*As Jesus and his disciples were on their way, he came to a village where a woman named Martha opened her home to him.* [39]*She had a sister called Mary, who sat at the Lord's feet listening to what he said.* [40]*But Martha was distracted by all the preparations that had to be made. She came to him and asked, "Lord, don't you care that my sister has left me to do the work by myself? Tell her to help me!"* [41]*"Martha, Martha," the Lord answered, "you are worried and upset about many things,* [42]*but only one thing is needed. Mary has chosen what is better, and it will not be taken away from her."*

THE SERMON

On this eighth Sunday after Pentecost, we come to the last sermon in my three sermon series on our Covenant Vision. Our vision at Covenant is: *"To be an inclusive community of faith 'Offering Hope + Showing Faithfulness + Sharing Joy.'"*

In the first sermon, we saw that the fulfillment of **"The Vision of Offering Hope"** means: *(1) Putting our Trust in Jesus, (2) Standing Firm in the face of Opposition, and (3) Offering Christ as the Hope for a Better Life.*

In our second sermon, we saw in Jesus' parable of the Good Samaritan and the actions of a Good Samaritan right here in Covenant that **"The Vision of Showing Faithfulness"** is accomplished by *(1) Bearing fruit in every good work, even when no reward is anticipated, (2) Being sensitive to the needs of the people we* *encounter, and (3) Having the compassion and the courage to act and to do what needs to be done.*

So those past sermons bring us today to the last point of our vision statement – **"The Vision of Sharing Joy."**

In the last section of I John 4:8, we find this simple but ever so important statement--*"God is love."* I believe a vision of sharing joy only becomes a reality in a church when the people of that church come to understand that *"God is love."* So let me share with you three points about how we use God's love for us and our love for God at Covenant to achieve **"The Vision of Sharing Joy."**

We must realize that model for sharing joy comes from God's love for us.

The famous English writer, G. K. Chesterton, once wrote, **"The Christian ideal has not been tried and found wanting; it has been found difficult and left untried."**[40] You and I know all too well that the reason the Christian faith is difficult is that we are called to love not only our family and friends (*which for a lot of us is a great challenge all in itself*), but we are also called to love our enemies, and those that do not like us, and even those who are willing to protest, loudly and publically, who we are. I got a first-hand experience of that last challenge this week. I must admit that I did not pass the test as well as some of our other church members.

---

[40] G. K. (Gilbert Keith) Chesterton, What's Wrong With the World (1910), Chapter 5.

On Wednesday morning, after I left morning prayers at Grace Episcopal Church, I was coming down First Avenue on my way to Brookwood and St. Vincent's Hospitals for visitations. As I approached our church, I noticed four people standing near the corner. I initially thought they were waiting on the bus, until I got close enough to see that they were protestors, standing there, reading the Bible aloud, with two of their protest signs posted on our property!! They were from *"Operation Save America"* formerly *Operation Rescue*.

Realizing who they were and what they were doing, I turned around and came back to the church. When I got out of my car, they just smiled at me. *(I think they thought I was coming to join them.)* I walked over to the signs, picked up one of their signs, and flung it out in the street. I was going to do the same with the other sign but decided just to crush it instead. One of the protestors started to come over to retrieve the sign from me and I told him **"if you step one foot on that grass, you go to jail. I am sure you know the rules, just as well as I do."** One of the women took out a camera and snapped my picture. I looked at her and asked, **"Do you want me to spell the name that goes with that picture?"**

Later in the day, Mary, Jeanette, and Elisa came to the Church, and they wanted to know if they could offer the protesters some comfort and hospitality. I had been to the hospital, returned and had cooled down by then, so I said of course it was okay to do so. Also, by that time, I had taken our *"Gay by God"* sign out front where they were protesting and put it on the top church step. So, Mary, Jeanette, and Elisa took chairs out to them *(to sit on the easement, not our property.*) They offered them water. Elisa offered to cook them some food but they refused. *(I am not sure they trusted the recipes she would be using.)*

Later, one of the men came over to Jeanette and asked her if she was a Christian and how long she had been one. Then he said to her, **"[t]here was a man here earlier in a collar, I assume that was your pastor."** She said to him **"Yes, he was. This is my church and I love my church very much."** He then said, **"He seemed upset. I do not know why he was upset."** She said to him, **"Well I do. I understand very well why he was upset."** The protester asked, *"Why?"* Jeanette replied**, "You don't know everything he has done for our community and the battles he has had to fight or the battles that our congregation as a whole has had to fight to protect those who want to be gay Christians."** She said, **"There is nothing you can say that will change my mind and nothing I can say that can change your mind, most likely."** She also said, **"Even Jesus once got angry in the temple."** He looked at her with a puzzled look and then said, **"Yes, he did"** and walked off.

Mary decided to share the joy of music to go along with their scripture reading, so she turned the speakers and monitors outward and opened the front doors and blasted praise music for them. Not long after that, they left.

In that exchange on Wednesday morning, you find my anger rising and I will admit my response was not the best course of action for me as the pastor of this church. However, while I do support people's right to protest, even those who disagree with me, you are not going to protest against me and use my property to do so. In Mary, Jeanette, and Elisa's actions, you find them living out the principles of **"The Vision of Sharing Joy."** Unlike me, they chose the better way.

In the gospel lesson today, Martha is all upset with her sister, Mary. Martha is busy doing things while Mary is sitting at the feet of Jesus just taking everything in that Jesus has to say as He is "Sharing Joy" with those in his presence. Martha complains to Jesus *"Lord don't you care that my sister has left me to do the work by myself?* Jesus said to her, *"Martha, Martha, . . .You are worried and upset about many things, but only one thing is needed. "Mary has chosen what is better."*

I do not think there was anything wrong in my actions on Wednesday, and I stand by them. However, if I had taken the time to really think about it, perhaps I would have interacted with the protestors differently. Nonetheless, I am glad that other members of Covenant--Mary, Jeannette and Elisa--were here, because they personified **"A Vision of Sharing Joy," based on the model of God's love for us.** They looked beyond the protest against our church and saw humans in need of human comforts. **They chose a better way.** That brings us to my second point:

Sharing joy requires us to remain connected to the source of love.

Our ladies' interaction with and toward the protestors showed that they were connected to the source of love. Our ladies gave the protesters chairs, offered them food and water, and played praise music for them. Our ladies responded to the protesters with acts of love and kindness. This kind of reaction is only possible when you are connected to the source of all love--God.

St. Frances de Sales, a Bishop of Geneva in the early 1600s and a Roman Catholic saint, is reputed to have said, **"What is so surprising is not solely the fact that God loves, what is so surprising is the full measure of God's love."** The miracle is not that we love God--the miracle is that God loves us. When we begin to get a glimpse of what that loves does in our lives, it begins to overflow and we cannot help but share it with others. In I John 4, John says in verses 11 and 12, *"Dear friends, since God so loved us, we also ought to love one another. No one has ever seen God, but if we love one another, God lives in us and His love is made complete in us."* That scripture illustrates what it means when we have **"The Vision of Sharing Joy,"** for when we have that vision, **we remain connected to the source of love–God!** When we remain connected to God's love, as the women of this Church did, our actions and reactions will be tempered by God's love.

Sharing joy requires commitment and sacrifice.

This year we had a very prominent role in the PrideFest activities here in Central Alabama and it was all because of the commitment and sacrifice of dedicated people here at Covenant. (*If you were a part of Covenant's participation in any way in Pride: marching, working on or riding the float, the pride dance, the interfaith service, staffing the Covenant booth or children's activities at PrideFest, or singing with the Choir at Pride, please stand up.*) **We**

thank you for your commitment and sacrifice to sharing joy with our community.

I also want to tell you that your commitment and sacrifice made a difference. Today I baptized little Joshua McGhee. Joshua was the first child to visit the children's activities area this year at PrideFest. Lisa Hayes, our children's church director, was on duty when he came by to visit. While talking to Joshua, Lisa asked him if he went to church anywhere. He replied *"Oh, no Ma'am! They don't let us go to church because my Mom's gay."*

Lisa asked him to sit down and talk with her. She told him **"God loves you and your mother just as you are and Jesus died for you and your mother just like He did for everyone else in the world."** Lisa told him that at our church we welcomed everybody and shared with him that she is gay and has a partner. He said *"Well, my Mom is the one that is kind of mannish."* Lisa laughed and said *"That is great. We would love for them to come to church."* She gave Joshua one of our church T-Shirts and asked him to go and show it to his Mom and her partner and ask them that if they got a chance, to please come by and talk with her before they left. Shortly thereafter, Adrian and her partner did come by. They wanted to make sure that if they came to Covenant, the preacher was not going to get them there and then start gay bashing them. Lisa assured them "gay bashing" would not be likely since he's gay also. After talking with them a little while, Lisa got Susan Green to escort them over to the Covenant Booth and the rest is history.

Covenant's preparation for and participation in PrideFest is always hectic. We spend long hours working on the float; we march in the parade; we present a mini-concert; and we sponsor a booth. It is tiring. Most of us are completely drained by the time the week is over. Sometimes, we even question why do we do all of these things. **But**, whenever I get a little discouraged, God reminds me that our commitment and sacrifice are for a purpose. Because we were at PrideFest, Joshua found us and we found Joshua. Today we baptized little Joshua and we now have three new members of our congregation—Joshua, Adrian (his mom) and Nadia (her partner).

Joshua, Adrian, Nadia, Lisa, Susan, and all of our members who supported PrideFest are excellent examples of what we mean when we talk about **"The Vision of Sharing Joy."**

1) **It is about modeling God's love for us, as Mary, Jeanette and Elisa did;**
2) **It requires us to remain connected to the source of love; and**
3) **It also requires commitment and sacrifice.**

Today, let us catch a vision of sharing that kind of joy with others as we sing of God's love for us that is "*higher than the mountain*" and that "*day after day. . .remains.*"[41]

---

[41] Motley, Mike. "Day After Day." Integrity's Hosanna! Music, 2001.

ABOUT THE AUTHOR

Rev. J. R. Finney, II, is the Senior Pastor of Covenant Community Church, Birmingham, Alabama, where he has served since September 2000. Affectionately known as "Pastor J. R.," Rev. Finney's career includes service in the United States Air Force, where he attained the rank of sergeant; employment as an accountant with the Memphis Light, Gas, and Water Company, Memphis, Tennessee; and Section Chief of Financial Compliance, Hazardous Waste Division, Region Four, for the Environmental Protection Agency (EPA), Atlanta, Georgia. Rev. Finney's career at the EPA spanned 17 years and he was serving as president of the National Treasurers Employees Union, Local 276, at the time he accepted his current position at Covenant Community Church. Covenant Community Church ministers to a predominantly LGBTQ congregation in Birmingham and Central Alabama.